I0153755

BAY OF BISCAY

THE BASQUE COUNTRIES

Scale of Eng. Stat. Miles.

Cap Machichaco
Cap Breton
Bayonne
Biarritz
Bidart
Pyrrhorade
Peyle
Baigts
Orthez
Salies
Sauveterre
Labastide
Hasparren
Bonloc
Iztürüz
St Palais
Navarreins
Mauléon
Oloron
Aramitz
Montory
Navarrenx
Monein
Portugalete
Guernica
Lequeitio
Bilbao
Elgoibar
Cestona
Loyola
Vergara
Durango
Villa Real
Deva
Ernani
Irun
Hendaye
Urrugne
St Pée
Cambo
Ainhoa
Bidarray
Ascarria
Ustaritz
Vera
Sare
Maya
Elizondo
St Etienne de Baïgorry
St Jean Pied de Port
Esnazu
Larrau
Ste Engrace
Pic d'Anie
Accous
Urdax
Aldudes
Valcarlos
Ahusky
Alsasua
Vitoria
Miranda
Tolosa
Pamplona
Puerto
Lizarraga
Burguete
Roncevaux
Pic d'Orhy
Ochagavia
Roncal
Soraueren
Aoiz
Pas Chalar

Spanish frontier
Railways
Carriage roads
Eastern limits of Basque country

BIARRITZ

AND

BASQUE COUNTRIES.

BY

COUNT HENRY RUSSELL,

MEMBER OF THE GEOGRAPHICAL AND GEOLOGICAL SOCIETIES OF FRANCE,
OF THE ALPINE CLUB AND SOCIÉTÉ RAMOND,
AUTHOR OF 'PAU AND THE PYRENEES,'
ETC., ETC.

With a Map.

LONDON:
EDWARD STANFORD, 6 & 7, CHARING CROSS, S.W.
—
1873.

INTRODUCTION.

It is almost as difficult to guide a tourist as a lover or a sinner, when the country which the author attempts to describe is not yet popular and famous, and no one can be sure that what *he* loves or admires in it will have the same favour with those who do him the honour of following his steps or advice.

This is, however, what I have undertaken in these pages, conscientiously, but most capriciously written during my long walks through the wild and romantic Pyrenæan regions, called "Basque country," a land of mystery, whose mountains have not always a name, and whose immaculate torrents, like the sweet, but rash follies of youth, fling their glittering waves over every sort of precipice, always looking for a level, which they never find on land.

There are a few places, especially on the

Spanish side, which I had to describe without
seeing them; but though I cannot agree with
a witty author, who thinks this is often an
advantage, my authorities for those places are
too respectable not to be fearlessly accepted.
They are: Adolphe Joanne's 'Itinéraire des
Pyrénées,' Mr. Murray's always truthful
'Handbooks,' my young friend Henry
O'Shea's 'Guide to Spain,' and Germond De
la Vigne's little book on Biarritz.

I therefore hope and believe, although
nothing human can be complete, that this
Guide will meet most wants: and to British
tourists who have a yacht I may also sug-
gest a journey from England to Bayonne by
sea, as yachts of all tonnage can enter its
harbour, whence to Biarritz it is only five
miles.

With these few words I leave the reader;
for Guide-books are like friends: they can
afford to be simple, as long as they are true,
and need not look solemn.

H. R.

London, *June*, 1873.

CONTENTS.

CHAPTER VIII.

CHAPTER IX.

CHAPTER X.

CHAPTER XI.

CHAPTER XII.

CHAPTER XIII.

CHAPTER XIV.

CHAPTER XV.

CHAPTER XVI.

BIARRITZ AND BASQUE COUNTRIES.

PART I.

CHAPTER I.

BIARRITZ.

Biarritz is a charming village, fast becoming a small town, and pleasantly situated on a cliff of the Bay of Biscay, at about 20 miles northeast of the mouth of the river Bidassoa, where the Atlantic coast becomes Spanish, and suddenly begins to run from East to West. On a clear day, the immense curve of this line of coast, which is very mountainous in Spain, but quite flat in France, can be easily traced with the naked eye from any hill round Biarritz, for a distance of more than 100 miles, the last blue hills in the "far West" not being far from Bilbao.

Biarritz is little short of 500 miles (by rail) from Paris, 423 from Madrid, and 67 from Pau. By leaving London in the morning,

B

you reach it the next day at one o'clock P.M.
The railway station is two miles from the
town, at *La Négresse.* (Omnibuses.)

A gayer little place it would be difficult to
find, even in midwinter. Twenty-five years
ago it was quite unknown, but now more than
forty English or Spanish families reside there
permanently; and in summer it suddenly
becomes as crowded and elegant as a German
watering-place. But its normal population is
not quite 4000. It is capriciously and irregularly built, the houses looking as if they had
fallen from the sky, the streets running up
and down, right and left, but at almost every
step letting you catch glimpses of the wild and
blue ocean between two houses, or above them.
It is the Bournemouth of the Bay of Biscay,
but with the sun and colouring of Italy.
There are trees in the streets—sycamores,
tamarinds, &c. The walls are so white, that
in summer their glare is as dazzling as snow.
No streets are paved, so there is no rattling of
carriages, and you hear no noise but the wind,
of which there is plenty, to say the least. . . .
It is indeed not like Pau in that respect.

It is far from easy to pass a fair judgment

upon the very changeable climate of Biarritz, as it varies not only during a given week or day, according to the wind, but sometimes from year to year, and to a strange extent. The contrast between its climate and that of Pau, which is barely 60 miles distant, is very striking. Whilst at Pau, which is so calm and tranquil, wind is almost unknown, the Biarritz atmosphere is as boisterous as any in Europe; and in favour of it, it must be admitted that the temperature is slightly higher than at Pau, especially in the evening and at night. It is well known that the ocean tends to equalize temperature. Snow is seen sometimes at Biarritz, but rarely; and when the south wind happens to blow, as it often does in the depth of winter, its burning blasts make the temperature run up to 70° (shade). The prevailing winds are from the west, south-west, and south, and they are by far the strongest. North and east winds (both very cold) blow but seldom. In clear weather the atmosphere is of such purity, that peaks fully 80 and 90 miles distant are seen to perfection with the naked eye; and from the top of the lighthouse the view extends from the Pic du Midi de Bigorre (E.S.E., 9439 feet) to Cape Machichaco, near Bilbao (W.); in all about 150 miles.

Nothing can be grander than an autumn sunset on the Bay of Biscay, seen from the Biarritz cliffs; the tints are both so warm and so angry, that sea and land seem on fire, and the clouds are awful to look at.

The ocean on this coast, where only two or three rivers can pollute it, is of the purest blue; it is never yellow or green. The temptation to bathe is therefore very great, and the water never being extremely cold, bathing is possible at all times of the year. But the surf is so great in autumn and winter, that the utmost prudence is required, since in fishing alone at least fifteen cases of drowning have taken place within the last three years, even at enormous heights above the sea.

There are three cold-bathing establishments, and a fourth for hot baths (Port Vieux). The sand on the beach, quite free from pebbles, is particularly fine and soft. It is also very porous, and dries up an hour or two after high water. The huge strand, which runs almost due north of the light-house, lined for 100 miles with green or dark pine forests, has all the strange splendour of a desert; and these pines do more than charm the eye; they are exceedingly useful in checking the advance of the sea, which used, before they were planted, to encroach on the land at an alarming rate every year, sweeping the sand-hills before it.

As for boating, it is seldom pleasant or safe on this terrible coast, and a ship is rarely seen on this angry wilderness of waters; still, a few sailing boats are to be had in the *Port des pêcheurs*, at the rate of 5 fr. for the first hour, and half that price for every succeeding hour.

There is a strange absence of sea-weed at Biarritz, and fish cannot be said to be very plentiful; the most common are tunny fish (often weighing 60 lbs.), soles, lobsters, and *dorades*. Countless multitudes of sardines are often caught a few miles farther south, and anchovies by millions, but seldom near Biarritz. Conger-eels are very abundant; they are caught at night, when they rise near the surface, and they are much relished by the natives of this coast.

HOTELS are many and splendid.

The *Hôtel d'Angleterre* (proprietor, M. Cam-

pagne) is a magnificent structure, 240 feet long,
with twenty large saloons, bath-rooms and
reading-room, a garden, interpreters for every
European language, and commanding a most
superb sea view. Strange to say, it was built
in one year! The best Spanish wines can be
had here, M. Campagne being also a wine
merchant.

The *Grand Hôtel* (proprietor, M. Gardères)
is also an enormous one, with the same view
as the other. In both of these hotels there
are *tables d'hôte* at all seasons.

The other hotels are: *des Ambassadeurs,
de Paris et Londres, de l'Europe, des Princes.*

Villas abound, and are let furnished at any
season. In summer prices are rather alarming; but the height of the bathing season only
lasting two months, Biarritz may be said to
be, for the rest of the year, as cheap a place (of
its size and importance) as can still be found
in Europe. During the winter it is eminently
suited to small fortunes. There are numbers
of houses (furnished), which can be had in
spring and in winter for about 100 fr. *per
month*, though during the season they fetch
the same price *per day!!* (But for informa-

tion on this subject apply to Victor Benquet, who keeps a public reading-room on the Place Ste. Eugénie; the best English and French papers, with a few Spanish ones, are always there, and a well-stocked lending-library.)

There is an English church, and a resident clergyman.

Biarritz also boasts of its *English Club* (near the Place Ste. Eugénie). The *Casino* is a wonderful place; but it only remains open for five months; and in winter its deserted terrace, swept by rain or hurricane, sadly reminds you of the lovely music and lovelier women who, a few months before, on warm autumn evenings, made you forget the splendid roar of the ocean, the hour, and every sorrow. It is a strange contrast indeed.

Still, even in winter, Biarritz is cheerful and lively. There are parties (dancing, dinners, &c.) at least twice a week. Several families entertain a good deal; and that the society of the place is increasing is proved by the graceful or sumptuous villas which are being built at both ends of the cliff, where the town extends in an undulating semicircle facing the west. On entering Biarritz by the north (as you come from Bayonne), you first behold on your right the Emperor's château, or *Villa Eugénie*, with its green fields and park (of which hereafter). On the other, or left side, you see an elegant villa, with slim turrets, now the property of the Duke of Frias. A little farther on, and on the same side, you come to a proud and imposing mansion, belonging to the Marquis de Javalquinto, which contains many fine pictures and other works of art. A few minutes after, you leave on your right a substantial, castellated building, the property of Mr. Bellairs, who also keeps a bank (*International* Bank). Just opposite (left) you pass *Sunny Side*, a most lovely villa of different styles, in which taste and imagination have accumulated and combined everything useful or beautiful in colouring and furniture. This exquisite gem is the creation and property of Mr. Henry O'Shea, author of the 'Guide to Spain.'

On the other, or southern side of the town, along the cliff commanding the whole Bay of Biscay, the visitor will first reach the *Villa Hamilton*, an Elizabethan house, built by Miss Hamilton, and visited by the Emperor. It is strikingly handsome, and the sea view from it is the best in Biarritz.

Close by, on the edge of the cliff, stands the lofty structure, built in the Basque style by the Countess of *Nadaillac*, as if to defy all the winds of heaven.

In the distance, on the wild and sandy beach which runs south towards Spain, the eye is attracted by a picturesque, Moorish-looking building, called *Marbella*. Lord Ernest Bruce owns it. It is a long mile from the town, has a glass dome of marvellous solidity, and a garden which makes it look like a refreshing oasis in a desert. The inside reminds one of the Alhambra court.

The *Goëland* must not be forgotten in a sketch of Biarritz. The view extends to every point of the compass, and it belongs to Count de Montebello.

Neither can we omit the *Bourguignon* house, with its charming garden, close to "Sunny Side." It was the property of a lady whom all loved and regret (Mrs. O'Shea).

Just beside the parish church (south-east of Biarritz) stands the *Grammont* château (M. Labat's), an imposing pile, with fine trees near it (a very rare ornament on this coast), and verdure all round. Napoleon III. spent two months there in 1854.

Lastly, near the light-house, and commanding all the country, the square house of the Marquis de *Noailles* looks from its cliff at half the Pyrenees and the boundless sea.

The VILLA EUGÉNIE, or Emperor's palace, is a very remarkable building, whatever architects may say of its faults. Its proportions and situation (to say nothing of the beautiful park, all created as if by magic, on a soil which used to look like the Sahara) make it exceedingly interesting, and certainly deserve admiration. It was begun in 1854, on the beach called *La plage des fous*, which runs north-east of the town towards the light-house. Two rocks, only 40 feet above high water, served as foundations: in fact, the spray is often blown over the whole of the terrace which extends before it. It is in the Doric style below, and Corinthian above.

It is open to the public on Mondays, from one o'clock until five.

The park (where 15,000 pines, six years old, were planted and thrive), the gardens and meadows, lake, &c., cover in all 30 English acres.

Do not forget to see the wonderful chapel built in the park, close to the Bayonne road. It looks Moorish, and glitters in the sun.

(*N.B.*—For all details concerning the Villa, see Ardoin's ' Souvenir de Biarritz.')

LIGHT-HOUSE.—It is certainly one of the curiosities of Biarritz, and well worth visiting, were it only for the panorama seen from the top.

Leaving the Bayonne road near the little chapel of the villa, you proceed to the left, gradually and gently ascending. After passing the *De Noailles* villa (left), look south-east, where the distant and snowy peaks of the Eaux-Bonnes, Cauterets, &c., begin to peer on the horizon, whilst the elegant light-house itself profiles just before you to the north-west, its snow-white column on the blue background of the gigantic ocean. It is just one mile from Biarritz.

You are allowed to enter, and, by giving a franc to the keeper, can ascend to its summit, until an hour before sunset. Its height (above its base) is 154 feet; but it is 220 feet from the mean level of the sea to the lantern, whose revolving light is seen at 16 nautical miles. No less than 256 steps lead up to it. The view is almost boundless, and the line of peaks from west to south-east is fully 150 miles in extent.

Here you are sure to see, in autumn and winter, even in the calmest and loveliest weather, such a stupendous swell as is never witnessed even on the west coast of Ireland. The mass, height, and length of these enormous waves are scarcely credible; they are hills of water, and their deafening roar is heard inland most distinctly at more than twenty miles! In fact, they make the coast tremble, and the rocks vibrate like bells. There is no place more treacherous than this for looking on or for fishing, as cataracts of sea water fly with the rapidity of lightning to an elevation where none could imagine he was not in safety; and ten or a dozen people have been drowned on this fatal headland within the last twelve years.

You can drive to the light-house by the road just described, and then walk back (at low water only) by the *Plage des fous* (S.W.) to the *Bains Napoléon.*

PORT DE REFUGE and PIER.—A wild scheme indeed, and which appears every day more and more hopeless. Napoleon III. suggested it, meaning to connect by a breakwater several of the detached rocks scattered on the north-western side of the *Port-Vieux*, and thus to form a small harbour, only open to the north. A clever engineer, M. Palaà, was entrusted with this almost superhuman undertaking: but the only result has been, after years of labour and more than one sacrifice of life, to accumulate a shapeless and useless mass of ruins along the intended harbour. The breakwater (or what is left of it) was built with concrete; artificial square blocks weighing 36 tons (some of them 48) were sunk by hundreds at random, and just where they liked to fall! But the tremendous surf has been playing with them, as if they were pebbles, and in 1868, one of them was carried right over the pier (22 feet above low-water mark) like a toy or a feather! For these, and for financial reasons, the works are now suspended. They have already cost 120,000*l.*, and all to no purpose. In fact, nothing human can resist such a sea as the sea of

Biscaye, except, perhaps, at *St. Jean de Luz*, where nature has half made a harbour.

ATALAYA.—Here the view is also marvellous. It is a sharp promontory, with ruins on the top, and to the north of the *Port-Vieux*; the word itself, *Atalaya*, meaning an "observatory," in Arab or Spanish. The *Semaphor* is close by, being both a station for the weather observations, and (in winter) the telegraph office.

Numbers of houses in the Basque provinces, when built on a height, are called *Atalaya*. The insignificant ruins on the Biarritz Atalaya are those of a fortified castle, which stood there in the twelfth or thirteenth century, and was meant to defend the harbour, Biarritz being in those times still a great place for *whale fishing*. Later, however, the "monsters of the deep" emigrated to colder latitudes, where the Basques pursued them. It is very seldom now that a whale is found or stranded on this coast.

In summer and autumn, when the population of this little town is doubled or trebled, the rocks and beach are alive with gay crowds speaking almost every known language. Between fifteen and sixteen thousand foreigners visit Biarritz during the summer months, and the fall of the Empire has not in any way diminished the well-deserved prosperity of this cheerful and famous place, whose climate, in all seasons, is more and more appreciated. No doubt, it is cold sometimes, it *may* freeze for a whole week, but seldom more.* In general, it is very mild, the great July heats being tempered by an often strong sea-breeze. The rainy months are March, and sometimes April. Healthy people prefer the climate to that of Pau, but it is too bracing and too windy for consumptive persons. The sun is *always* hot.

DOCTORS.—Here are the names of the medical men now (1872) practising at Biarritz :—

English : Dr. Girdelstone.

French : MM. Adéma, Vicomte de Vauréal, Jaulerry, Affre.

---

* According to Dr. Ottley's comparative table of temperatures for 1863-4, it was generally about 4° (Fahr.) warmer at Biarritz than at Pau (in winter); but it rained less at Pau.

SHORT EXCURSIONS ONLY REQUIRING ONE DAY.

CHAPTER II.

BAYONNE.

It is five miles (by the high-road) from Biarritz to *Bayonne*, a handsome and wealthy town of nearly 27,000 inhabitants, situated on both banks of the river *Adour*, and four miles from its mouth. Within its walls the river *Nive* falls into the Adour. An omnibus starts from Biarritz every hour (in winter) for Bayonne, and every half-hour in summer. It is a pleasant drive of about 40 minutes, the road being lined, first with plane-trees, then with poplars, and passing (at the third kilomètre) before the gate of the charming and most fantastical *Villa Sophia*, belonging to M. Salvador, a Spanish gentleman. This villa is entirely "Moorish," and is covered with the most elegant arabesques.

A handsome bridge thrown over the Adour,

and made of stone, connects Bayonne with its suburb of *St. Esprit*, peopled mostly with Jews of Portuguese and Spanish origin, an intelligent and energetic colony, which settled there in the sixteenth century. The bridge is 840 feet long, and there are four other smaller ones on the Nive.

The Adour has its source in the Hautes-Pyrénées, at a height of 6000 feet, on the southern slopes of the *Pic du Midi de Bigorre,* and has a course of about 150 miles, but can scarcely be called navigable for more than about 40 miles above Bayonne. There used to be steamers from this city to *Dax:* but they have ceased to run, since the railway made them useless.

The Nive springs in the Basque country, and flows nearly due north for about 50 miles, before mixing its green and clear waters with those of the Adour in entering Bayonne. Bayonne to Pau by rail = 63 miles. There are three trains every day, both ways. Bayonne is a bishopric and a sous-préfecture.; Pau, as the capital of the " département," being the " préfecture.". And of all second-class *cathedrals,* Bayonne has probably the finest. It is its

c

proudest building. This Gothic edifice, begun
in 1141, and endowed in 1847 with an income
of 1400*l.* a year by M. Lormand, has a magnificent altar of white Italian marble, and the
sanctuary is paved with slabs of *blue* marble.
The stained glass and organ are also both very
remarkable.

The church of *St. André* has two graceful
spires (Gothic).

Bayonne is, in some parts, rather gloomy, its
streets being narrow and dark (a useful pre-
caution taken against the fierce July sun), but
it is very clean, has fine shops, and an unmis-
takable air of wealth about it, though its trade
by sea has sadly declined for two reasons:
first, the competition of the railway, and
secondly, the slow, but sure and continual
filling up of the *Barre,* or mouth of the Adour,
where sand is accumulating to an extent daily
more alarming, notwithstanding all precau-
tions, and every effort to prevent it. It is
indeed a sad prospect for this once flourishing
sea-port. The *maximum* depth on the "Barre"
is now under 20 feet, which is worse than unsafe, with a surf rising sometimes to twice that
height!

Still, there *is* wealth in Bayonne, as the number of imposing country villas scattered all round it abundantly testifies. Its articles of trade are chiefly wines, Spanish wool, resinous matter, wood for building, &c. Its hams and chocolate are famous.

The *theatre* is a fine building. Behind it (west) extends a " place" where the garrison band plays on Thursdays and on Sundays ; and here interesting observations may be made on the dress and features of the generally handsome inhabitants, whose Basque, " Gascon" or Spanish blood has engendered a mixed and most pleasing type of grace and manliness, seldom found united. The " grisettes " are nowhere so pretty. There is something "Andalusian" about them.

The British *Consulate* (— Graham, Esq.), is on the south side of this " place."

The *railway terminus* is on the right bank of the Adour, in the suburb of St. Esprit, where frowns the stern *citadel*, worth visiting for the view's sake, and in honour of the *Cimetière Anglais*, where were buried the 800 victims of the sanguinary sortie made in 1814. Bayonne only having opened its gates during the armistice, kept its proud motto, *nunquàm polluta.*

The history is most interesting. It is a very old city, and once belonged to the Romans, who called it *Lapurdum*, had a fleet there, and made it very strong. In fact ruins of Roman works are still found in it. Then it was plundered by the Normans, Visigoths, &c., finally lost its name itself, and became *Bay-unna* (from *Baya ona*, two Basque words meaning "a good bay"). Later it passed (by the marriage of a Plantagenet with Eléonore de Guienne) into the hands of the British, and it was the last place (save Calais) which they possessed in France. Bayonne was retaken by the French in 1451, its governor and all the garrison becoming prisoners of war.

Vauban built the present citadel, and all the works now surrounding Bayonne, a "place forte" of the first class, however powerless it would certainly be against siege-guns of modern calibre. In fact every part of it is overtopped by hills, within range of large guns, and so useless is the fortified wall supposed to be, that it is likely to be soon demolished, the very dense population imprisoned within it having no longer room to move, and but little air to breathe.

Visitors limited as to time ought certainly to walk down the beautiful *Allées Marines,* on the left bank of the Adour. The trees, though cruelly mutilated in 1814, have now recovered all their original splendour, and for miles you can walk or drive in the shade, with the noble river on your right, and before you a conical and picturesque hillock, dark with pines, from the summit of which (three miles from Bayonne) the view, on sea and Pyrenees, is grand in the extreme. Just behind this hill are the ocean and the mouth of the Adour, or *Barre* (four miles from Bayonne), a perfect "hell" of roaring waves in bad weather. Opposite is *Boucaut* (right bank).

(For the road from the *Barre* to Biarritz, see Chap. III.)

It was in these angry waters that in 1814 eight British boats perished with almost all their crews, in entering the Adour. (See Napier, book xxiv., chap. 2.)

The mouth of the Adour has often been displaced. In the thirteenth century, it was

at *Cap-Breton* (12 miles farther north, see
Chap. XV.). In the following century it seems
to have been 12 miles farther still to the
north. A great storm in the sixteenth century
forced back the stream into its old channel.

There are steamers now and then, from
Bayonne to the Spanish coast (to Bilbao, San
Sebastian, &c. The office is quite near the
British consulate), and occasionally to Monte
Video, where the Basques emigrate in such
vast quantities. Cod-fishing in Newfoundland
is still kept up by Bayonne sailors.

HOTELS: St. Etienne, du Commerce, de la
Providencia, des Ambassadeurs, &c.

DILIGENCES daily to all the Basque country:
some start from the Hôtel des Basques (near
St. André), others from the *Porte d'Espagne*
(south of the town). But they are very bad.
The diligence "service" to Pampeluna by the
Port de Maya (south-east of La Rhune, 63
miles,) was stopped when the railway by San
Sebastian was completed: still they do run
sometimes, but irregularly.

No Englishman crossing Bayonne will fail
to give at least a glance at the splendid mansion which, from the hill on the other side of

the Adour, makes every building in the country look small. It is Lord Howden's house, called *Caradoc*, and large as a palace, containing many art treasures, and commanding a splendid view which it is impossible to describe.

For the battles on the banks of the *Nive*, south-east of Bayonne (Dec., 1813), see Napier, book xxiii., chap. 2. In five days' fighting the French lost 6000 men, and the allies upwards of 5000, five English generals being wounded.

The brave English soldiers who fell in the furious sally from Bayonne (April, 1814), are buried in the *Cimetière Anglais*, near the citadel. This sortie cost the French 900 men and one general; the British and German loss amounted to 830 men. (See Napier, book xxiv., chap. 5.)

CHAPTER III.

THE "REFUGE" AND THE "BARRE."

IT is a little less than five miles from Biarritz
to the "Barre," or mouth of the Adour (N.E.).
You can either follow the long, straight beach,
north-east of the light-house, and walk three
tiresome miles on sand, or else take the carriage road, leaving the light-house on your
left. Here on the cliff if the traveller look
south-east on a clear day he will see 80 or 90
miles of peaks. At half a mile beyond the
light-house the main road turns to the right,
near a pretty chapel, and a sandy cart-road on
the left leads, in ten minutes, to the once romantic "*chambre d'amour*," an ugly hole, now
half filled with sand, where two lovers were
once overtaken by the sea, never to be heard
of again. (Maidenhair fern.)

There are small inns close to the "chambre
d'amour," and bathing-houses on the beach.

At a mile beyond the light-house (two from
Biarritz) you come to a sort of village, or

group of scattered houses, called *Cinq Cantons.*
Here, on a triangular "place," with a pretty
kiosk on the left, the road divides; take the
left branch, the right one leading (two short
miles) to *Anglet,* on the Bayonne and Biarritz
road.

After a few minutes you will observe on
your right a pile of buildings, with the blue
Pyrenees far away behind. This is the *Refuge,*
always open to visitors. It is barely two
miles and a half from Biarritz. Here were
the head-quarters of Wellington in 1814.
Founded in 1839 by the Abbé Cestac, a most
zealous and venerable priest of Bayonne, this
pious community of penitent women has succeeded beyond all hope, materially as well as
morally speaking, for the wild plateau of barren
sand bought by the abbé has become, in his
hands and under his careful direction, the
most fertile land in the country. All Biarritz
has tasted the milk and the butter of the
"Refuge." A beautiful kind of embroidery
is also made here. (See Lawlor's 'Pilgrimages
in the Pyrenees and Landes.')

The road continues north, leaving the
Refuge on the right, and soon divides, on

entering a dismal pine - wood. The right
branch leads to Bayonne, crossing a strange
region of pines and sand-hills (*dunes de Montbrun*), a solemn solitude, where no noise is
heard but the moan of the wind and the roar
of the sea behind, falling in cataracts on the
distant and empty beach with a kind of
metallic sound. If you follow *this* road
(*Montbrun*), thus giving up the *Barre*, which
remains to your left, you reach the top of a
sand-hill, with a grand view of the Pyrenees
in the south-east. Close by, on your left,
quite hidden under the trees and lost amongst
the sands, is a convent of *Bernardines*, nuns
recruited partly from the "Refuge," whose
whole life is spent in the culture of this sort
of desert and in prayer. It is a very severe
order; they never speak, and walk bare-
footed. They might be taken for ghosts, and
their holy abode is silent as the North Pole.

Shortly after passing on the right of this
convent (which you do not see) the *Montbrun*
road descends, and finally meets the left bank
of the Adour, just at the end of the *Allées
Marines*, at a distance of four miles and a half
from Biarritz, and one mile and a half from

Bayonne. By Montbrun it is therefore six miles between these two places.

But if you wish to see the *Barre*, you must follow straight on (north) when you enter the pine-wood. Two good miles from here (not five from Biarritz) will take you to the *Barre*, where the Adour rushes into the sea. There is a small light-house, and a long latticed pier (made of wood), meant to deepen the main channel of the river, by straightening it, and thus accelerating the current; but nothing will avail; the sand is accumulating every day, and only ships of very small tonnage can now make their way to Bayonne.

From the Barre to Bayonne is four miles, always on the left bank of the river. From Biarritz to Bayonne, passing by the Barre, it is therefore a little under nine miles. You can drive the whole distance, and through Montbrun also.

BOIS DE BOULOGNE.

This little tour of not quite five miles in all is very attractive, and may be taken in a carriage.

Leaving Biarritz by the parish church
(half a mile south-east), you follow the main
road to the railway station : but before reaching it, on entering a pine-wood, you must
turn sharply to the right (west), and leaving
on your left both the Madrid railway and a deep
lake or pond (*Lac Mouriscot*), whose blue waters
glitter beautifully on sunny days, you plunge
into a wood of oaks, cork trees, and tall pines,
where for a few minutes you might imagine
you were crossing Canadian solitudes. It is a
most romantic spot, and pretty wild flowers
abound. On the lake there are boats for hire,
for in spite of the coldness of its waters, there
is plenty of fish in them. Subterranean com-
munications are supposed to exist between
this lake and two others, described hereafter
(see p. 29).

On the hills opposite, behind the railway,
there were fierce engagements in 1813.

The wood on this side (north) of the lake is
so sheltered that it scarcely loses its leaves.
The road now gradually turns to the right,
towards the sea, between which and the Lac
Mouriscot Napoleon I. once thought of dig-
ging a canal, navigable to men-of-war !

At last you completely turn round, facing the north, and leaving on your left the very beautiful château of *Marbella* (Lord Ernest Bruce), you re-enter Biarritz by its southern side and cliffs.

LAKES BRINDOS AND MARION.

They are both very small, and the former (*Brindos*) has shores as wild and dismal as can be seen or imagined. But lake *Marion* is surrounded with trees, and in summer its green banks are cool and pleasant.

The walk to both these lakes is about five miles in all, going and returning.

First go to the Biarritz railway station (two miles), or rather, go near it; but before reaching it you turn to your left, on the Bayonne and Madrid road, which you follow for about half a mile. You then leave it, turning to the right on a generally very muddy footpath. In ten minutes (on foot or riding), you reach the boggy shores of lake *Brindos* (only a few acres), a deserted and silent sheet of water, on whose brown and barren banks scarcely a tree is to be seen.

After a few minutes of melancholy contemplation, you will be too happy to leave it, and to retrace your steps towards the Bayonne and Madrid road, where you will return a quarter of a mile towards the station, and soon find a pretty carriage-road branching off to the right (N.W.). This will take you in ten minutes to the sheltered and green basin where the waters of lake *Marion*, protected from the wind, reflect their banks like a looking-glass. They are as calm and transparent as the eyes of a girl of seventeen summers.

Follow the north side of it, and in a few minutes (half a mile) you meet again the road by which you started, at a mile south-east of Biarritz, between the parish church and the railway station, and quite close to the former. (You can drive the whole distance, with the exception of half a mile, before coming to lake Brindos.)

N.B.—Most of the following excursions being through Basque territory, we had better devote a few chapters to a general description of this strange land and race.

CHAPTER IV.

N.B.—The whole of this chapter is translated from a French manuscript, kindly placed at my disposal and written by the Rev.—— Haristoy, parish priest of Sauguis, near Tardets.

THE BASQUES.—THEIR ORIGIN, MIGRATIONS, STRUGGLES, TERRITORY, POPULATION, &c. &c.

THE Iberians, both those of the Euxine and those of Spain (whether the latter descended from the former, or the former from the latter, *sive hi ex illis, sive illi ex his oriundi sint*, Menoch., Genesis, chap. x., v. 2) descended, according to the most learned historians, both religious and profane, from *Thubal*, the fifth son of Japheth, who was himselft he third son of Noah.

Authors are unanimous in fixing the time of their arrival in Spain, or in *Sethubalia* (which in Basque means "land of the sons of Thubal"), as early at least as the fifteenth century before the Christian era, since the Phenicians, who at that time penetrated into the peninsula, found them already established there.

Now, ancient authors, as well as modern ones, like Oyhenart, G. de Humboldt, Ampère, Amédée Thierry, &c., consider the Iberians as the ancestors of the Vasco-Cantabrians. The primitive names of several towns in Bethica (now Andalusia) have Basque etymologies perfectly justified by the topographical position (present or past) of those towns. As M. de Montglave has properly observed, the words or names of " Ararat," " Armenia," " Sinai," " Sem," " Bethulia," " Phasga," &c., mean " there," " close by," " oath," " son," " full of flies," " pasture land," &c., &c. M. Mentelle also tells us in his 'Dictionary of Ancient Geography,' that " the *Cantabrai* s a river of India, which Pliny counts among the most considerable which fall into the Indus." These different places therefore seem to show us the successive stopping places in the migration of the Vasco-Cantabrians, from east to west.

Pushed back by the Phenicians and Celts, by Rhodian and Phocean colonies, the Vasco-Cantabrians probably settled in that part of

Spain called later by the Romans *Taragonensis,* in the regions which have now become the provinces of Asturia, part of Old Castille, of Guipuscoa, Biscaye, and Navarre, and the northern districts of Aragon and Catalonia. (Diodorus of Sicily, Silius-Halicus, Ethicus, cosmography, &c.)

The above-mentioned authors, and likewise the geographer Strabo, Pliny, &c., give us interesting details about the customs, bravery, and countries of the Vasco-Cantabrians. Roman history shows them to us struggling with the Carthaginians, with the Romans also, for more than two centuries; and neither armies of the two great rival cities ever succeeded in reaching the interior or heart of Cantàbria; for in spite of the verses of the servile Roman poet (Horace) who, although admitting the Cantabrians were unconquerable "before that time," *Cantaber non antè domabilis,* attributes to the Emperor Augustus the glory of having subjugated them, the Cantabrians were neither beaten nor submissive. In proof of which Tiberius, son-in-law and successor of Augustus (A.D. 14), was obliged, in order to secure their alliance, to

D

promise to respect their institutions, and their autonomy. Vespasian also granted all the Cantabrians the right of *Latium*, and Caracalla that of Roman citizenship.

The Vasco-Cantabrians did not remain on the southern side alone of the Pyrenees; they made a passage for themselves through the immense forests of that chain, by a conflagration mentioned with the exaggeration characteristic of Greek authors (Diodorus of Sicily, and Denysius of Halycarnassus). Several names of Pyrenæan localities remind us of this conflagration; and those of Illiberris, Elusaberris (Eause), Bigorra (capital of the Bigorrians, *Bigorrienses*), Elimberris or Ilumberris (capital of the *Auscorrum*), &c., are indicative of unquestionably Basque etymologies. That is, why Amédée Thierry, after Humboldt, &c., does not hesitate to affirm that "the most ancient monuments of geography show us the Iberian race occupying the great isthmus made by Gaul between the Gulf of Gascony *. and the Mediterranean. The arrival of the

---

* It is well known that Strabo called the Gulf of Gascony Cantabrian Ocean (*Oceanus Cantabricus*), and de Marca calls it the *Basque Sea.*

first tribes of Gauls pushed back the Iberians towards the south; but the topographical names, such as are found in old Spain, prove the long stay, on the south side of the *Garonne* and almost as far as the Loire, of a population speaking the Iberian idiom, of which the present *Basque* language is a still living remnant."

Cæsar and other ancient writers had observed the analogies of language and customs which existed between the Cis-Pyrenæan and the Trans-Pyrenæan inhabitants, as also the differences existing between them and the Gauls, the Celts, and the Belgians.

These *Vasco-Cantabrians* of *Aquitania* followed Hannibal at Trasimene, at Cannes, &c. They defended their country against the invasions of the Cimbri and the Teutons. They fought beside their Trans-Pyrenæan brothers against the Romans under Sertorius, &c. When helped by their ultra-Pyrenæan brothers (for the dangers threatening the Cantabrian confederation always united them), they had to fight against the Roman legions commanded by Crassus, lieutenant of Cæsar; the *Venearni,* the *Monensi* (Moneins), the *Osquidates* (of

Ossau), the *Illuros* (Oloron), the *Sybillates* (Soule), spoken of by Pliny, are not mentioned amongst the people who sent their submission and gave up their hostages to the young lieutenant, then the master of Northern Novempopulania. On the contrary, Cæsar tells us that "a few petty people higher up in the mountains, *paucæ ultimæ nationes*, did not make their submission, and sent no hostages, being emboldened by the advanced season and the approach of winter." It is no doubt proved that the Cis-Pyrenæan Vasco-Cantabrians, when they saw their brothers beyond the mountains entering into an alliance with the Romans, towards the time of Tiberius, did admit *de jure* the Roman domination, for there was a Roman cohort at Lapurdunum, &c. (Bayonne). (The word Laphurdunum is Basque, and means "land of briars and water." In fact, formerly all the plains of Labourd, like those of Soule and of the Pyrenees, were lakes or morasses, and there are proofs of it.) But it is equally proved that the Vasco-Cantabrians on both sides of the Pyrenees *have always lived* (and under all dominations) according to their *fueros*, or old

customs: the ultra-Pyrenæan ones until 1841
(for the privileges which they enjoy now are
but remnants of their ancient *fueros*), and the
others until 1789.

The Vandals, Herules, the Alains, the
Suèves, &c., who came towards the year 409
from the banks of the Rhine, did not pene-
trate into the Vasco-Cantabrian country,
neither did the Visigoths. The Franks of
Clovis did not reach lower Novem-populania,
consequently not our present countries. On
the contrary, the ultra-Pyrenæan Vasco-Cantabrians, who had already made several de-
scents upon the Adour basin, themselves
pressed by the Visigoths in the Alava country
and its neighbourhood (*Navarre,* "land of
valleys"), tried to profit by the quarrels of
Clotaire II. with Théodoret and Thierry, kings
of Austrasia and of Burgundy. They therefore came down from their mountains, and
joining their Cis-Pyrenæan brothers, they
carried their conquests as far as the Garonne.
(Frédégaire, chap. xxi., 54.)

What must explain the rapidity of these
conquests was that the Gallo-Romans of
Novem-populania were first enervated by the

softening civilization which the victor's policy
had inoculated, and then tired of the vexations
and oppressions of the "masters of the palace,"
chiefs of the second race of our kings. To
those times must be traced back those entrenched camps known under the name of
Casteras, or *Touronac*, which are found in our
countries and in lower Novem-populania. It
is by mistake they are attributed to the
Romans, whose camps differed widely from
these.

The Vasco-Cantabrians did not at once settle
down in the invaded territories as an homogeneous nation, when with their families they
brought their laws, their customs, and language. They made sure their conquests far
into Novem-populania, whose inhabitants had
no difficulty in accepting and admitting the
supremacy of the Duke of the Vascons. They
strengthened their conquests by garrisons, by
Basque colonies, organized in militia forces.
Proofs of this can be found both in those entrenched camps and in the names, plainly and
exclusively *Basque*, of several places in Novem-
populania. For instance, Harriet, Biscaross,
Itchous, Auzour, Arsa, Arrion, &c., &c.

(These names are taken amongst many, and literally, from a map of the Government of Guienne and Gascony, printed in 1700, by H. Gaillot, geographer to the king.)

Their conquests once made sure, the Vasco-Cantabrians established themselves as an homogeneous nation behind the line of *Aramitz* (*Ara-Ametz*), *Oloron* (Il-ur-on, " city of good water "), *Naverreinx* (Nava-erri), and *Sunarte* (Sauveterre). It is behind this line that they principally fortified themselves, and that we see them stand invincible against the armies of the Carlovingian kings. The new-comers settled especially in unclaimed lands between Labourd and Soule, which, in memory of the original country of its inhabitants, was called Basse-*Navarre*. Novem-populania, which after the name of the conquerors of the seventh century had been called *Vasconia*, preserved that name even after the retreat of the Basque colonies, flying before the armies of the second race of kings, towards the mountains, and behind the above-mentioned line. Just as beyond the Adour the *patois roman* changed the word *Vasconia* into *Gascogne*, and as *G*uillaume came from *W*illelmus, so among

the Basques the name of *Vasconia* was changed
into that of *Basconia*, from the habit of pro-
nouncing V like B, which made the witty
Scalier say : "Felices populi quibus *vivere* est
bibere."

FRENCH BASQUE COUNTRY.

It is formed by three distinct provinces or
"cantons" : the western one is called *Labourd*,
the eastern one *Soule*, and the central one
Basse-Navarre. Formerly, as we said above,
it was limited on the north by the Adour, on
the south by the Pyrenees, on the west by the
ocean, and on the east by the line which from
Aramitz, passing through Oloron, Navarreinx,
Sunarté, Sauveterre, went to meet the Adour.
At a later period, whether on account of en-
croachments by the Béarnais, or because the
Basques retired, the territory occupied by the
latter was curtailed on the east. Moreover,
as both the French and the Spanish govern-
ments are bent upon the eradication of the
Basque tongue, the circle within which it is
spoken is getting daily more limited.

Here are *exactly* the limits of the *French*
Basque country, in other words, a list of the

last villages beyond which the language spoken is the *patois* of Béarn or Gascony. Basque is spoken in the under-mentioned villages, going from west to east : Bidart, St. Pierre, d'Irube, Lahonce, Urcuit.

From north to south: Bardos, Ayherre, Orègue, Charitte-Alixe, Ilharre, Arbouet, Sussaute, Arbérats, Etcharry, Arouë, Charitte-le-bas, Arrast, Larrory, Mendibieu, Hôpital St. Blaise, Esquille, Haux, Ste. Engrace.

Biarritz and Bayonne were formerly Basque towns, as the name *Bi-Arritz* (" two rocks ") proves it for the first; as to the second, its original name of Lapurduna, *Lapa-Ur-Duna* (meaning "a pool"), or *Lapar-Ur-Duna* (" land of briars and water "), and its second name of Bayonne, given to it towards 1132, *Baia-Ona* (" good bay "), prove it clearly, even if we had not also the authority of Esteban de Garibay (*Compendio historial d'España*), book iv. chap. iv. It must be observed that the Bay of Bayonne was better than now, when the Adour used to fall into the sea *near* Cap-Breton.

As to the village of *Anglet*, it is recent, and owes its name to a military post created there by the English when they possessed Guienne.

The French Basque country is formed by four valleys, having each its river, which crosses it in a direction perpendicular to the great mountain chain from which they descend. The most westerly of these rivers, the *Petite Nive*, or *Nivelle*, flows through the Labourd country, and meets the sea at St. Jean de Luz. The second is the *Nive*, and the third the *Bidouze*, which both fall into the Adour, the first at Bayonne, and the second near Guiche. . . . . . The fourth river of the French Basque country is the *Saison*, which crosses the Soule country, and falls into the Gave of Oloron, near Sauveterre.

The three provinces of Labourd, Basse-Navarre, and Soule, had until 1789 their "general assemblies," or "states," and customs peculiar to themselves.

According to the last census, the *genuine* population of the French Basque country does not exceed, in all, 120,000 souls. There are 47,000 in Labourd, 46,000 in Basse-Navarre, and 27,000 in Soule.

SPANISH BASQUE COUNTRIES.

1. NAVARRA (*Nava-erri*, "land of valleys"), having Pampeluna for capital, has a population of about 300,000 souls. The kingdom of that name, founded in the ninth century, successively passed, through female descent, since 1234, into the hands of the houses of Evreux, of Aragon, of Foix, and lastly of Albret. It was usurped in 1512 by Ferdinand, King of Aragon, from the house of Albret, which only kept the *Mérindad* of St. Jean Pied de Port.

The chief towns are Pampeluna, Tudela, Olite, Estella, *Sanguera*, the town of St. Francis Xavier, apostle of the Indies. The father of this great saint was from Iatxou, near St. Jean Pied de Port (Basse-Navarre).

2. BISCAYA, having for capital Bilbao. Population of the province, about 130,000 souls. Bilboa (or Belvao) was built in 1300 by a prince of Biscaya, on the banks of the river called in Basque *Ibaïçabal* (" wide river "), or in Spanish, Nervion. The ancients called this river *Chabyls*. Its water was famous for the tempering of arms. That is

why the *Cantabrians* thought nothing of the arms whose iron had not been tempered in the Chabyls.

Bilbao lies in a fertile plain. The chief towns on the coast are *Bermeo*, or Bermejo, with a good harbour, and famous oranges. *Portugalete*, on the banks of a river. *Larédo*, built by the Goths, on a height surrounded on all sides by rocks, with a harbour below the town. *San Antonio*, with a harbour also.

The inland towns are *Durango*, in a deep valley, between lofty mountains: its inhabitants excel in working iron. *Hellorio*, in a pleasant and fertile valley. Its halberds were much esteemed, and its inhabitants still work iron most ingeniously. *Ordugna*, in a beautiful valley, everywhere encircled by steep and high mountains. *Lanestosa*, in a very similar position.

3. GUIPUZCOA; capital, *Tolosa*. Population of the province, about 130,000 souls. Tolosa lies in a pretty valley, at the junction of two rivers, the Araxe and the Oria.

The chief seaport towns are: *Fontarabia* (*Fons rabidus*, or *Ocaso*, in Latin), built in amphitheatre on the slope of a hill; besieged by the French in 1638. *Irun* ("good town," in Basque), with a handsome church. *Renteria*, a picturesque village. *Passage*, a small town opposite the village of *Lesso*. *San Sebastian*, a city of pleasure and good living. *Gueteria*, built on a hill, birth-place of John Sebastian del Cano, who was the first to go round the globe, after three years' navigation. The Emperor Charles V. gave him as an armory, a globe with this inscription: *Tu primero me rodeaste. Zumaia, Deva*, formerly important in the times of whale fishing. *Motrio*, &c.

The chief inland places are: *Villafranca* and *Segura*, two handsome towns on the banks of the Oria. *Mondagron*, famous for its medicinal waters. *Placencia*, on the smiling banks of the *Deva*, and known for its fabrication of war weapons. *Bergara*, called the "shop of Mars." *Azpeïtia*, in a very pretty valley, containing within its territory *Loyola* and *Onis*, which both belonged to the family of St. Ignatius of Loyola. See the convent or house of St. Ignatius. Lastly, *Heybar* and *Helgoybar*, owing their importance to gun foundries.

4. ALAVA; capital, *Vittoria.* Population of the province, about 86,000 souls. Vittoria was founded by Sanche, King of Navarre, in a very fine and rich valley.

The chief towns of this province are: *Trevigno,* perched on a hill; *Pena Cerrada,* lying between very high mountains, &c.

The three sister Basque provinces, after having had their own lords till the thirteenth century, gave themselves up to the Kings of Castille, accepting them as their masters.

AMUSEMENTS OF THE BASQUES.

1. *Pastorals* or *tragedies.* The Basque language possesses about forty tragedies or pastorals, borrowed from the Bible, from mythology, from ecclesiastical or profane history. They are acted in the public squares, by young or even old men, in costumes, and very numerously attended. These compositions, full of stirring scenes, which M. de Montglave has compared to the comedies and tragedies of Aristophanes and of Sophocles, are far indeed from being the creations of poets "who knew neither how to read or write." The authors

of many of them are well known, and we believe their origin cannot be traced back beyond the fifteenth century.

2. *Toberacs*, and in the Soule language *Cinzarroxacs* ("noise of little bells"). They are "*Charivaris*," fallen, it is true, into disuse, meant to stigmatize a second marriage, or conjugal infidelity. They are held during the month or months preceding the second marriage, or as long as conjugal infidelity is talked of, and at night, in the neighbourhood of the house of the betrothed, but at a respectful distance. It is there that one or two *Coblacari*, in the most awful din of bells and ox-horns, &c., try the patience of the betrothed by versified dialogues or songs, full of malicious allusions, &c.

3. *Tobero-munstracs, Asto-lurterracs*. They are also a sort of carnival, which only differs from the preceding ones by the solemnity given to it, and by the place where it is held. To say nothing of all the disorders arising from them, the expense of these "charivaris" prevents their taking place very often. When they are held, it is in the public squares, before an enormous gathering of people, col-

lected there from every corner of the Basque country.

4. *Mascarades.* They must not be confounded with those carnivals which sprung from the *Bacchanalia, Saturnalia,* &c., of the Romans. These mascarades, still in honour in Soule, are only pantomimes. . . . They existed in Spain and France ages ago.

5. *Dancing.* If we were to believe a certain Pierre de l'Ancre, a Boileau, a Hamilton, &c., " Basque priests dance, and are the first to go to the country balls. . . . A Basque child knows how to dance before knowing how to call his father and his nurse ! . . . Joy begins with life, and only ends at death !!! " &c., &c.

These are indeed historians (not history) bravely quoted by certain authors, because it pleases them to write without knowing what they write about !

What is certain, and proved beyond dispute, is that dancing (always excluding the mingling of sexes, except in the presence of fathers and mothers) formerly existed among the Basques, as an honest amusement and a bodily exercise. But modern dances, which I will call horrible pantomimes, have as yet no name in our language, and are happily unknown in our valleys, still free from the ignominies of modern civilization.

6. *Jeu de paume* (hand-ball). *The* really and exclusively national game of the Basques is the *jeu de paume :* and there is no village, however poor or isolated, without its *rebot,* where not only young, but middle-aged men, in presence of the whole village, play with a passion only equal to their agility, vigour, and suppleness, those games so disputed and popular. . . . . . These sports sometimes bring together five, ten, and even fifteen thousand Basques from both sides of the Pyrenees, as for instance during the glorious days of the *Gascoïna,* in Spain.

CUSTOMS OF THE BASQUES.

There are a thousand accusations, both foolish and unfair, current against the Basques. . . . . The Basques are not " superstitious," but " religious," which is not the same thing. . . . . All the efforts of Jeanne d'Albret, &c., have failed to introduce a single Protestant

E

notion here. . . They are civil and kind . . . they address you uncovered, and always salute you (save in towns). They most willingly leave their fields to guide or direct travellers, and expect nothing more than a thankful acknowledgment. . . They are also hospitable. . . and in their houses, always wonderfully clean, they at once give the " place of honour " to a stranger, in the secular seat called *çuçulia*, which has been there for centuries near the hearth, and will thus pass to all future generations. For the night, they are sure to give you the best room they possess. . . . .

Whatever may have been the causes which first induced the Basques to emigrate to America, it is now an established fact, that almost every Basque family has one or several of its members on the banks of the Rio de la Plata. But we cannot shut our eyes to the great amount of money they send home; to say nothing of those " Americans " who, when they return, enter, by marriage, into the best houses of our country, or build those splendid houses often seen in Labourd, &c.

They form homogeneous populations in many parts of America, especially at Buenos-Ayres, where they now have their own priests, churches, &c.

HARISTOY,
Parish-priest of Sauguis.

E 2

CHAPTER V.

THE BASQUES.

THE preceding chapter (IV.), written by a Basque himself, shows the antiquity of this mysterious race; but when and from what land it first came to Europe, is a problem which history alone will perhaps never solve, although numberless volumes have been written about it.* According to Humboldt, the Basques really were the first inhabitants of Spain. Abyssinia, Carthage, South America, India, are some of the countries from which they are supposed to have slowly migrated. Perhaps geology may help to clear this much-agitated question.

The Basques were probably of Iberian or Cantabrian origin, and preceded the Celts by twenty centuries. They were called *Euskarians*, when the Phenicians came, in the year 1100 A.D. Numbers of them are now quite fair, and most of them are tall; so their type appears to have much changed since Tacitus,

* See the work of *Chaho*.

who described the Iberians as brown men, with frizzled hair. In any case, they differ widely from what Voltaire cynically called them—"*Un petit peuple qui saute et danse au haut des Pyrénées*"!!

The Basques are certainly not less than 3000 years old, and as far as we know they were never conquered. Neither the Celts, Vandals, Romans, nor Moors could make them yield. Later, they resisted and checked the armies of Clovis. They had excellent weapons; their sword was adopted by the Romans, and Horace praised their shields. Lucan says the Pyrenæan Iberians were "the terror of the world." (See *Chaho.*)

Besides history, many of their customs prove their antiquity; and in the Basque language (*Escuara*), which is unhappily fast dying out, Biblical traditions are often quite plain, *viz. Semé* means "son" (*Sem,* Noah's son), &c.

The origin of this extremely old and mysterious language is little known, so different is it from all idioms ever heard of. Sanscrit has some analogies with it. Here is a specimen of a Basque word:

Azpilcuetagaraycosaroyarenberecolarrea, which means, "Lower field of the high hill of Azpicuelta." Stuttering is hopeless for a Basque.

There are many idioms or dialects in Basque, as the Spaniards often misunderstand the French. It has been said of the Basques, that they write " Solomon," and pronounce it " Nebuchadnezzar " ! !

Wherever they came from, these bold mountaineers certainly are a most manly, adventurous, honest, and handsome race, numbering at present, according to an excellent authority (Francisque Michel), about 840,000 (700,000 in Spain alone). This seems, however, far beyond the number. They love the sea beyond all things, and are first-rate sailors. It is almost beyond dispute that they discovered the coasts of North America. Nomadic and restless, they emigrate in thousands to the Rio de la Plata; but their deep love of their country almost always carries them home again as soon as their fortune is made. There are about 100,000 Basques in South America. Inland, they are eminently a pastoral people.

Their strength, agility, and endurance are proverbial : " To run, to jump like a Basque," is a common saying all over France. They are also very persevering. In fact, they are, with the Bretons, the most manly of all Frenchmen.

It does one good to live with men so cheerful and honest. Very reserved at first, until they know you well, they soon become inquisitive and familiar, but always respectful. As for drunkards, beggars, or thieves, they are almost unknown in this happy country.

Patriarchal, but warlike, the Basques are also an eminently religious people, and deeply Catholic. Their churches (where the sexes are always separated) are both large and handsome, and quite full on Sundays. Very often these buildings have strange steeples with three points, supposed by many authors to represent the Blessed Trinity: this, however, is much disputed. A thousand stentorian voices, singing in unison under those sacred roofs, shake the walls, and prove that the Basques possess strong lungs as well as religious fervour. In fact, there is a sort of wild energy in every action, thought, or impulse of this powerful race, far superior to the lazy Gascons and more or less effeminate Spaniards living around it in the same climate.

A Basque is always active. If he is not labouring in the fields, he will spend hours in his tennis-court, playing the *jeu de paume* with as much energy as if it were a battle-field. Every Basque village has its *jeu de paume,* where the French and Spaniards meet in hundreds or thousands, till one side finds its Waterloo.

Dancing and all athletic sports are in universal esteem; but at dances the sexes are always kept apart, just as at church. Then in autumn the Basques have "pastorals," played in the open air (see Chapter IV.). Accoutred in fanciful costumes, the performers are on horseback. The subjects are taken from Scripture, or from Tasso, Dante, &c. The prophet Jeremiah once appeared with the Crimean medal!!

Though the language is rich and harmonious, the literature is said to be rather meagre.

Amongst the old and strange institutions of this very peculiar race, we must mention the "Assembly of States," called *Bilsar* in times gone by—*Bilsar* meaning strictly "assembly of old men," like the Latin *senatus* (*senum cœtus*).

"It is in woods of ancestral oaks that land-owners and heads of families used to meet and settle the administrative rules of all the communes. There, standing with their backs to the ancient trees, leaning on their medlar-tree sticks, they discussed, deliberated in perfect liberty, and they took decisions which more than once compelled the kings of France and of Navarre to yield to their *fueros* (privileges). Two rocks served as a seat for the president and his secretary; whilst another block, roughly polished, was the table upon which were engraved the decisions arrived at.

"The origin of the *bilsar* is lost in obscurity, but it is believed to have preceded the establishment of Christianity among the Basques. What gives a great foundation for this opinion is the fact that priests were excluded from it, though the country was deeply religious; no doubt it was thought objectionable to modify the original constitution which ruled public affairs."—(*Cambo, &c.,* by O. Duvoisin.)

Physically, the Basques are tall and muscular, but, above all, supple and swift-footed; they are indefatigable pedestrians. In their eyes there is both energy and haughtiness,

though blue eyes are common among them.
The women are superb, and have beautiful
hair. The Basque type seems a mixed one
and we may mention as a very strange fact,
which seems to be well authenticated, that as
late as the year 1790 specimens of real savages
were found in the forest of *Iraty.* Gipsies are
numerous.

A curious stick, called *makila,* is used all
over the country. Made of the medlar-tree,
it is often worth more than a guinea. There
are plenty to be had at Bayonne.

Here are a few Basque words, which may
be useful in travelling :—

Bread—Oguia.
Wine—Arnoa.
Water—Ura.
Salt—Gatza.
Pepper—Bipherra.
Breakfast—Gosaria.
Dinner—Bazcaria.
Table—Mahaina.
Spoon—Golharea.
Fork—Sardesca.
Plate—Gathelua.
Knife—Ganibeta.
Glass—Gandola.
Cup—Kikera.
Soup—Elcecoa.
Beef—Idikia.
Mutton—Cikitekia.

Veal—Aratchekia.
Fowl—Oilokia.
Milk—Esnia.
Sugar—Azucrea.
Tea—Dutia.
Butter—Burra.
Cheese—Gasna.
Eggs—Arroltceac.
Potatoes—Lur-Sagarra.
Brandy—Aguardienta.

Pear—Udaria.
Apple—Sagarra.
Cherry—Guerecia.
Grape—Mahatsa.
Orange—Iranya.
Lemon—Citroina.

Strawberry—Marhubia.
Salmon—Izokina.
Trout—Amarraina.

Chair—Kadera.
Bed—Ohea.
Door—Bortha.
Key—Gakhoa.
Window—Leihoa.
Candle—Gandera.
Inn—Ostatua.
Horse—Zaldia.
Donkey—Astoa.
Dog—Zakhurra.
Rat—Garratoina.

Fire.—Sua.
Firewood—Errekina.

Gold—Urrhea.
Silver—Cilharra.
Copper—Cobrea.

Mountain—Mendia.
Forest—Oihana.
Road—Bidea.
Grotto—Harpia.
Flower—Lorea.
Monday—Astelehena.
Tuesday—Asteartea.
Wednesday—Asteazkena.

Thursday—Ortceguna.
Friday—Ortciralea.
Saturday—Larunbatea.
Sunday—Igandea.
To-day—Egun.
To-morrow—Bihar.
Yesterday—Atzo.
Morning—Goiza.
Evening—Arratsa.
Night—Gaua.
Never—Nihoiz.
Always—Bethi.

Rain—Uria.
Snow—Elhurra.

Hot—Bero.
Cold—Hotz.
Pretty—Pullit.
Ugly—Itsusi.
Young—Gazte.
Old—Zahar.

Man—Guizon.
Woman—Emastea.
Boy—Muthicoa.
Girl—Donceila.
Child—Haurra.

Large—Handi.
Small—Ttipi.

EXTRACTS ON THE BASQUES,

Taken from the 'Penny Magazine' (1842).

".... The Basque language is generally supposed to be totally different from all the European languages, an assertion from which entire assent may be reasonably withheld for the present. .... If we are to believe the Basque grammarians, their language existed before the building of the Tower of Babel, and was brought to Spain by Tubal. Setting aside such extravagances, it may be remarked that the testimonies adduced to prove that the Basque language was spoken by all, or nearly all the primitive inhabitants of the Peninsula, are so numerous and conclusive, as to amount almost to a demonstration. .... The number of Basque words existing in the names of places in Italy (of which Orvieto and Urbino may be quoted among others), is perhaps a sufficient proof that some of the inhabitants of both these countries once spoke the same language. .... The Basques were the only Spaniards who preserved their independance, not having been subdued by any of the nations who invaded the Peninsula. Pompey was the first who in the year 60 A.D. led the Roman legions into that country; but the passage of Strabo quoted to prove that he built Pamplona, was evidently not intended by the author to signify anything of the kind .... no less obstinate was their resistance against the Goths. ....

"The government of the (Spanish) Basque provinces differs entirely from that of the rest of the Peninsula. Every province has its own constitution and a separate government, not differing much in spirit and form from each other. The people of Alava, at a very remote epoch, which some historians suppose to have been prior to the invasion of the Arabs, appointed their civil and military governors at a general assembly. This assembly met every year at the Campo de Arnaja (?), a plain near Vitoria. It was composed of the bishop and archdeacon, of all the secular clergy of the province, and all the principal men; including also ladies, who were the representatives of their families. .... In the year 1457, at an assembly held at Rivabellosa, by order of Enrique IV. of

Castile, a collection of the laws and privileges of Alava was formed and approved; and by that code they are governed at present. . . . .

"There is no building belonging to the state; and even the prisons belong to private individuals, who let them to the state. The people pay only one direct tax, which consists in a moderate rate for every house, and is equally divided; so that the rich and the poor contribute to the state the same sum. The revenues of the Church are so scanty, that the richest abadia, or rectory, is not worth more than 140*l.* per annum.

"The chief privileges of the Viscayans consist :—

"In paying no taxes except those levied by their Juntas.

"In every Viscayan Hidalgo, or 'gentleman,' (and acknowledged as such in every part of Spain) not being subject to any tribunal, or to any other laws (either in their own province or in any other part of the Peninsula) than their own, and in having a judge resident in Valladolid for the administration of those laws in cases occurring out of the province.

"In being exempt from military service, except in the defence of their own country.

"In the enjoyment of commercial liberty; and finally, in not having any officers appointed by the government of Madrid, except the masters of the Post-office.

"The Basques of the three provinces (Spanish) also contribute to the royal exchequer a certain 'voluntary donation.' . . .

."The Viscayans and Guipuzcoans are the best sailors in the Peninsula, and skilful in commercial transactions. They are very active and industrious. Their chief occupations are agriculture, commerce, and the manufacturing of iron. The women assist the men in the cultivation of the ground, and are remarkable for their cleanliness. Their manners are simple and easy; they are fond of dancing at their festivities, and enjoying the moderate pleasures of the table.

"Their national instruments are the tambourine and the bagpipe. Their dance is quick and lively, and is always accompanied by singing. In their weddings they greet the bride in going to and coming from church, by firing guns and pistols, and very often she is induced to fire them herself.

"In some villages, after the burial ceremony is over, they distribute bread, cheese, wine, and walnuts among the persons invited; and some beg money to pay for masses for the release of the souls of the deceased from purgatory.

"The dress of the men and women is similar to that of the mountaineers of Castile: both wear a species of shoe which is made of a hard and untanned piece of hog-skin, or that of any other animal, which they soften by soaking it in water, and then cut it into pieces of the size of the foot, which they fasten on by strings.

"The Basques are in general frugal, cheerful, honest, and courteous, without meanness. When kindly treated, they are docile and manageable, but if they are dealt with severely and harshly, they become stubborn and intractable, and it is for that reason that they are with great difficulty subjected to severe military discipline, particularly by officers who are not of their own country. Gonzalve de Cordova, from the experience he

had of them in Sicily, often said that he
would rather keep lions than Viscayans.
They are a brave people, and better adapted
for a system of guerilla warfare than any
other nation in Spain."

CONCLUSIONS OF THE REV. W. WEBSTER, UPON
THE BASQUES.

(See *Société Ramond's* Bulletin of April, 1872.)

" These points we think may be regarded as
more or less definitely established :—

" (1.) That the Basque or Escualdun race, a
people of many tribes, was very early settled
in Spain, in the south of France, in Corsica,
and in Sicily.

" (2.) That they are the race more or less
vaguely designated by the Greeks as Iberians.

" (3.) That Celtic races immediately succeeded them, overlaid, and to a certain extent
mingled with them, as the Celtiberi, &c., of
classical authors.

" (4.) That the Basques were established
in their present position in France long an-
terior to the sixth century, A.D.

F

" (5.) That the Basque language (Escuara) belongs to the Turanian family of languages; either to the Finnic branch, or to the North-American Indian.

" (6.) That the Basques, instead of being a darker, are, on the whole, a fairer people than any of their neighbours.

" (7.) To these may perhaps be added, that the form of the Basque skull is peculiar. . . .

" Wherein lies the interest of this question: Who are the Basques?   In this, that it is, in some sort, a crucial problem for philology and ethnology.   Philology declares the Basques to be a Turanian race.   Their present physical features, excepting the alleged small capacity of the cerebrum, present one of the finest types of the Indo-Caucasian race.

" The problems to be solved are these: Have the Basques, by the influence of climate or civilization, changed in physical features from a Turanian to an Aryan type? or have they, originally an Aryan race, in some way acquired a Turanian language?   Or, have all Aryan races gone successively through a monosyllabic, agglutinative, and inflexional form of language; but the Basques stopped short, like the Turanian races, at the agglutinative stage? Or, has the change in their physique been simply the effect of intermixture with Aryan, Semitic, and especially Celtic blood?

"Can these questions be satisfactorily answered? We think not, at present. . . . . Are they likely to be so in future? Or is the problem insoluble? We answer hopefully; but we think the solution is to be sought rather from Anthropology and prehistoric Archæology than from any fresh light to be drawn from historic records. To us it seems that in the Basques we have, as it were, an older stratum of our race, one once widely spread, now only cropping up through the posterior and overlying strata in one corner of the Western Pyrenees, and probably somewhat metamorphosed in its passage through the incumbent and neighbouring strata; but we have some slight indications in the classical authors of its presence on the surface in older times, in other localities. We believe that it is still possible for the three youthful sciences of comparative Philology, pre-historic Archæology, and Ethnology, to determine with

more or less exactitude the place of the Escualdun in the history of mankind, and no slight
aid towards this result we think will be given
by the work which we have just reviewed."*

* (*Note au sujet de l'ouvrage de M. Bladé sur l'origine des
Basques, par* M. W. WEBSTER.)

CHAPTER VI.

BASQUE COUNTRY.

THOUGH its boundaries are very vague, at least in Spain, the Basque territory is much larger than is generally supposed. In Spain it consists of *Navarre, Guipuzcoa, Alava, Biscaye,* and part of *Asturias,* and contains, according to Francisque Michel, about 700,000 inhabitants. In France it is nothing like so large, and much less populous (140,000 inhabitants. See Chap. V.). But its limits are better defined; you always know when you pass them. It is composed of *Soule, Labourd,* and *Basse-Navarre.* (See map.) Altogether, the Basque country, including French and Spanish provinces, is about as large as Wales.

The land is very green, undulating, and picturesque, some of the hills being upwards of 6000 feet high; and if you reach any height, no matter where, you are certain to get an extensive and varied view of mountains and plains, and often of the sea, besides

streams and beautiful rivers, such as the Nive,
Adour, Bidassoa, Bidouze, &c., which irrigate
green plains as rich as any in England. If
you stand on the plains, far from the Pyrenees,
at Biarritz for instance, you get an immense
view of mountains, forming a long, jagged
line of 150 miles. Then there are countless
villages, with their handsome churches and
walls of dazzling whiteness, with strange
blood-red lines on them. The Basque archi-
tecture is very peculiar. Now and then
you come to old manors covered with ivy,
and belonging to what are called " Americans," the name given to wealthy Basques
who have made their fortune in South
America.

Basque villages are not compact and regular; they are rather a disorderly accumulation
of houses scattered upon a very large surface,
without forming streets. The inns are always
clean, very cheap, and well supplied; but
French is seldom understood. Wood, in some
parts, is fifteen times cheaper than at Pau or
Bayonne.

On the whole, the Basque coasts are wild
and barren, very like Connemara or Donegal;
but on the hills inland you will find the largest

forests in the Pyrenees; you can travel 30 miles in some of them (*Iraty*, for instance), and have very good sport; there are bears, wild boars, wolves, and izards; quails, fig-peckers, partridges, thrushes, eagles, bustards, and wild ducks, &c., &c., besides the *palombes*, or ring-doves, wonderfully fast birds, which come in thousands in the autumn, and are caught in huge nets, as they attempt to cross the Pyrenees.

The wild singing swan has been seen, but seldom, during extremely cold winters.

There is trout in all the streams, and salmon is common in the Bidassoa, the Nive, &c.

There is nothing in France more beautiful than the Basque Pyrenees; and the only unpleasant thing to be said against them is the changeableness of the weather, a misfortune common and peculiar to most countries placed between mountains and the sea. The climate is maritime, wet and boisterous. It is more than redeemed, however, by the scenery, the exquisite verdure of the foliage and fields, and the graceful undulations of the soil, which give the whole country the rich but pastoral aspect of a great English park. Only lakes are wanting. Some peaks (those above 5000 feet) are very bleak indeed, and snow-capped for six months in the year; but even there vegetation and cottages are still found at very great heights.

It is a populous country, although there are no large towns. Houses are always in sight. There is no Basque village without at least one very neat little inn, where you are sure to get good beds, mutton, fowls, and eggs, besides game in the season, and at very low prices—an excellent dinner coming to a shilling! In fact, with five francs a day, pedestrians can cross the Basque country in every direction. It is perhaps the cheapest place in all Europe. With 10*l.* to spare, a good walker could easily explore it all in about three weeks. The average distance between two villages is about 20 miles. So you need not take provisions. All you want is a map (*État-major*), a compass, and a stick. You can send on any luggage you may want by the diligences, which cross every road in the country; but a knapsack is indispensable in the wild regions touching the Pyrenees.

Autumn is by far the best season for travelling, being mild and clear.

The roads are excellent; there is such a network of them, that a carriage can reach almost any locality, on both sides of the Basque Pyrenees; but if you want to cross the chain from France to Spain, you can only drive over in two places, along the coast, or from Bayonne to Pampeluna, by the *Maya* col, east of La Rhune. However, in a few years a road for carriages will probably ascend the Col de *Roncevaux.*

These fine hills are best suited to good pedestrians, who, without being enthusiastic mountaineers, disdain monotonous walking on straight or level roads. But, strange to say, a good guide is in these Pyrenees almost indispensable, perhaps more so than in the loftier and snowy parts of the main chain, where you can so often at one glance, by standing on an isolated summit, survey in the morning all the details of the country stretching like a map under your feet, study an entire province before exploring it, and make your way accordingly. In this intricate mountain region, where very few summits rise to any great height above their immediate neighbours, you can more easily get lost than in the Alps, because you seldom see very far before you, and your horizon is both confused and limited. Then the Basque hills are grouped with great irregularity, so that the countless little valleys which descend towards the plains seldom go straight for more than two or three miles, but wind their way down capriciously like long snakes. They are as tortuous and numerous as veins in the human body; in fact, you never steer for more than half an hour in the same direction. Besides this, there are immense forests, where if once lost in a mist, you might wander hopelessly for a week; and dreadfully narrow gorges with banks running down, at unpleasant angles, into furious torrents. A good guide is therefore advisable.

Better have a passport, which may be sometimes asked for near the Spanish frontier.

Always make friends with "gendarmes" and "douaniers"; for they might become unpleasant enemies.

As for "diligences," the reader can take it for granted that one or two are sure to run daily between all the towns mentioned, if a road connects them. Prices are very low.

CHAPTER VII.

CAMBO.

FEW people spend a day at Biarritz without visiting the pretty Basque town of Cambo, and the *Pas de Roland*, close to it. There is a carriage-road to both; and a rather dislocated kind of vehicle, pompously called a "diligence," goes daily from Bayonne to Cambo, starting from the southern end of the town (*Porte d'Espagne*).

Cambo lies to the south-east of Biarritz, just at the foot of the Pyrenees; and you have the choice of three roads, all good for carriages:—

From Biarritz to Cambo by Anglet, 15 miles.

From Biarritz to Cambo by the Négresse railway station, also 15 miles.

From Biarritz to Cambo by Bayonne, 19 miles.

Most people go by Anglet, as the road is better than by the Négresse. You take the Bayonne road as far as the fifth kilomètre (three miles), where you turn to the right, on a rather bad road for two miles, until you cross the railway to Madrid, and enter the Bayonne and Pampeluna first-class road, at two miles and a half from the former. You then go due south, through an undulating and picturesque country, where little woods alternate with great moors, and with the blue and intricate line of the Basque Pyrenees before you. You hear the Atlantic roaring behind you.

After leaving on your right a conical and wooded hill (*Ste. Barbe*), worth climbing for the view's sake, you suddenly find yourself on a high elevation, with the lovely basin of *Ustaritz* and the winding *Nive* under your feet. You then descend to this important Basque village (11 miles from Biarritz), whose walls are as white as Carrara marble, and glitter gaily in the sun. It is fully a mile long, and has a handsome church (Gothic). All the shutters are green or red; everything looks neat, comfortable, and gay; in fact, you guess at once you have entered the Basque country. Population, 2327 inhabitants.

There are many "Americans" at Ustaritz,

that is, as we have before said, Basque colonists who have made a fortune on the Rio de la Plata, and then come home. Here and there you see mills and manufactories. Salmon is abundant in the river.

It was at Ustaritz that the last Viscounts of Lapurdunum (Bayonne) ended their days; and it is in a grove of most venerable old oaks close by that the "general assemblies" of old men (in Basque *bilzar*) used to meet. The president and his secretary alone sat on a rock, whilst the members each stood gravely against a tree. (See Germond de Lavigne's '*Biarritz*,' &c.)

At a mile beyond Ustaritz, you leave on the right the road to *Pampeluna* (53 miles from here; and a few minutes after you pass under the walls of an imposing building (right), the *Laressore* seminary.

Then you soon come to the last hill before Cambo, and ascend it by a most gentle and graceful curve. (Here, if on foot, you can take a short cut to the left, and save half a mile.) Look back at the charming and green valley of the winding Nive, with the snow-white walls of Ustaritz smiling on its banks,

and here and there a light bridge joining them.
On your left, far below, you see the foam of
the "rapids," called *Nasses.* The whole scene
is like a great park, with blue Scotch hills,
and the sky of Italy.

At last you reach *Upper* Cambo, and another
mile takes you down to the *Lower* or *Bas-
Cambo*, where you find a good hotel, close to
the Nive (*Saint Martin*). You are here 14
miles from Bayonne and 15 from Biarritz (by
the way you came).

The *Négresse* road is rather bad in some
places for carriages. You go to the railway
station, cross the line, and then ascend a little
hill beyond; after which, leaving on your
right the *Arcangues* and *St. Pée* road, you
travel east, parallel to the Madrid and Bayonne
railway, which runs on your left. At three
miles from the Négresse (five from Biarritz),
you meet the Bayonne and Pampeluna road,
at three miles from the former and ten from
Cambo. After this you go on as above.

If you go to Cambo from Biarritz, by way
of Bayonne, the distance is 19 miles, and you
then have the choice of both banks of the
Nive. If you take the *left* bank, you leave

Bayonne by the *Porte d'Espagne* (south) and the churchyard, and soon pass (one mile) the ruins of *Marrac*, sold to Napoleon in 1808, and burnt in 1825. At Marrac Napoleon obliged Ferdinand VII. to abdicate.

Three miles from Bayonne take you to the junction of this and the preceding road, where you enter the Basque country. But if you take the *right* bank of the Nive, you must start from Bayonne by *Mousserolles*, its south-eastern suburb (left bank of the Adour). Crossing the Pau railway, you soon go through *St. Pierre d'Irube* and several fine estates, after which, leaving on your left the main road, which goes to Oloron, take a narrower one, and go south. Passing the great salt-works (three miles) of *Villefranque,* then the village of the same name, you will reach *Ustaritz* in about the same time as by the left bank of the Nive. (From Ustaritz, see above.)

Cambo is a village of about 1500 inhabitants, covering much extent on both banks of the beautiful *Nive,* perhaps the clearest stream of all the Pyrenees, and here a noisy torrent, as wild as a youth just escaping from school.

Even after leaving its mountains, and entering
a comparatively level country, it is almost as
restless as ever, and is only rendered navigable
by the help of man. Wherever the river is
shallow and wide, part of its bed has been arti-
ficially contracted into a narrow space, only
two or three feet wide, where the waters rush
furiously, like "rapids" in miniature, through
a kind of corridor, between two walls of
palisades. These rapids are called *Nasses*, and
through them boats shoot down quite safely
like arrows. Accidents *do* happen, but seldom.
The *Nasses* can even be ascended: but it thus
takes seven hours from Bayonne to Cambo, and
only two to go down! (distance by water,
about 16 miles). It is, however, an expensive
journey, costing at the least 20 francs.

The word "Cambo" comes either from
"Campus," or from the Celtic *Cam* ("a curve").

There are remains of an important camp
called, as usual, "Cæsar's," at a mile S.S.E. of
the town. Its Roman origin is very doubtful; still, it bears the traces of a very clever
system of defence, and 20,000 men could have
entrenched themselves in it.

The Pyrenees begin just behind Cambo,

and make it a lovely place, but they are very low, the highest point being under 3000 feet. The charm of this popular spot chiefly consists in its verdure, its woods, its peace and seclusion from every noise of the world, and its calm and mild atmosphere, scarcely ever disturbed by the gentlest breeze. It looks like a nest under a mountain. The leaves are quite green till November, and though no wind can ever blow strongly in such a sheltered place, the influence of the hot south wind and its fiery blasts often makes it almost too warm in midwinter; because, before reaching the Basque country, it does not sweep over snowy deserts and cool itself, as it must do at Pau, and most places north of the Pyrenees.

The bathing season (sulphurous and ferruginous baths) lasts till November.

(The bathing establishment is in Lower Cambo, quite near the Hotel St. Martin.)

You should not fail to go and see the view from the churchyard (Upper Cambo). The post-office is in Upper Cambo, and some hotels, at a height of 200 feet above the sea-level. Very good chocolate.

Salmon is abundant in the river, trout also;

and the fishing season lasts from the 1st of February until the end of October.

The waters of the Nive often rise in spring or in autumn, fifteen or twenty feet, and the floods are fearful. See the mark of the highest level reached, on the wall of the bathing establishment (June, 1856).

Out of the season Cambo contains nothing but Basques; but in summer, it is full of strangers, and amongst its illustrious visitors, we must mention the two Napoleons.

The shade and the verdure almost every-where found both in and around this charming place, make it doubly pleasant after Biarritz. But it is a pity that you cannot, even on foot, (except by scrambling) ascend the banks of the river, to the *Pas de Roland*. You can only follow them up for a little distance. Turning your back to the hotel, and taking the left bank, you walk for a little while on a tolerable footpath, well sheltered from the sun, and through immense ferns, with here and there a tall foxglove, but the track comes to an end after a short mile. If you wish to go on, you must here leave the Nive, and ascending a few minutes to the right,

you soon find two houses, near one of which
(that on the left) the track continues west,
with a good view to the south. Now the
road gradually turns northward, and takes
you back, after a steep descent through stones
and ferns, to your starting-point. It is a
walk of about two miles and a half, and perhaps the best thing you could do at Cambo,
if you have only an hour or less to spare.

But if you have time, you should certainly
go to the PAS DE ROLAND. It is a tall and
wild rock, with a great hole running right
through it, on the left bank of the green and
deep Nive, whose waters perhaps once crossed
this strange orifice or made it; but an absurd
and popular legend attributes it to the famous
Roland, the paladin of old, who kicked the
rock, and with his boot or sword thus opened
a passage for himself.

You can now drive to the Pas de Roland.
Leaving Upper Cambo on an excellent road,
and going due south, through a hilly country
full of pretty villas and cherry-trees, you come
to the village of *Itsatsou* (two miles and a half),
with a very rich church. You then enter
a sad and rugged gorge, with, however, some

splendid chestnut-trees, which soon cease; mountain scenery here begins in earnest. The Nive is on your left, and its emerald-green waters are transparent as glass; you can almost count the rocks forming black spots at the bottom, at depths of twelve and fifteen feet. Four miles from Cambo, you reach the *Pas de Roland.*

The carriage-road stops here; but you can walk along the Nive to *Bidarray* (six miles, see Chap. XVI.), and so follow it up to its very sources (37 miles from here. See Chap. XVI.).

Cambo to *Hasparren,* seven miles; to *St. Jean Pied de Port,* 25 miles. (You drive both.)

With half a day to spare, travellers to Cambo may ascend (on horseback or on foot) the easy *Pic de Mondarrain,* only seven miles distant, and rising 2460 feet, nearly due south of Cambo. It is a conical and bare but very *popular* mountain, seen from almost everywhere in the Biarritz country, and un-mistakable.

You go to *Itsatsou* (see above), and then begin to rise, at first under the shade of oaks and cherry-trees, but very soon in a great wilderness of ferns, passing near a ferruginous spring. Two hours and a half from Cambo, will place you on the top, where the view is splendid, combining a vast extent of sea and plains, with mountains. On this windy summit, are ponderous ruins of what must once have been (thirteenth century) an imposing and useful fort, the walls being five feet thick. Battles, in fact, were probably fought there, and a passage south of it is called "the defile of bones," a sinister and significative appellation! The rocks are quartz, limestone, and clay-slate.

In 1813, the French had a battery there.

By going down a little more westward than the preceding route, and following a stream, you can reach *Espelette* (Hotel du Mondarrain), whence to Cambo, three miles.

Espelette is a large village of 1500 inhabitants, on the first-class international road from Bayonne to Pampeluna, only 14 miles from the former. It is a wealthy place, and in a most charming country. See the church and *château*, once belonging to the Counts of Espeleta, a very old family, finally settled in Spain.

CHAPTER VIII.

ST. JEAN DE LUZ.

St. Jean de Luz is on the Bayonne and Madrid Railway, and eight miles from the Biarritz *station*, but ten from the *town*. All trains stop there.

It is a strange and melancholy, but picturesque town, of now 8000 inhabitants, or even less, though it once had four times that number. Now fallen and silent, it is all full of glorious " souvenirs." It existed in the sixth century; *Lohitzun*, its Basque name, meaning " a marsh."

Hotels :—De la Poste (on the right as you enter by the road); *de France* (near the church); &c.

It is very well paved, well built, and clean; but its chief attractions are the country surrounding it, the mountain of *La Rhune* (see Chap. XIII.), in fact, the scenery and walks. For half an hour is enough to dispose of the church, where Louis XIV. married, of his house, and that of the young Infanta he chose for his wife (1660).

A good pedestrian will prefer walking back to Biarritz (10 miles), and must even do so, or drive home, unless he waits for the late evening train to Bayonne. He can save a mile by taking a bye-road which turns to the left on the top of the hill of *Bidart*, a village four miles from Biarritz, and where you leave the Basque country. But on the western side of the Bois de Boulogne and its lake (see Chap. III.), there is a treacherous morass or bog, with pools beneath, not very safe when it gets dark.

You can also walk from Biarritz to St. Jean de Luz by the sea-side; but it is thus 15 miles instead of 10, and after *Guétharry*, unsafe for a lady. The four first miles of sand to Bidart are only fatiguing; but there you meet a first obstacle in the shape of a little river, to cross which you must lose ten minutes, the bridge being inland. Then, beyond *Guétharry* (two hotels, five miles from Biarritz), the coast becomes alternately very precipitous and cut up into bays, where you have to double the distance (even before

high water), and make weary semicircles in
yielding sand. In fact, it is better, and far
shorter, once you pass Guétharry, to ascend
and follow the summit of the cliffs; but even
by this route you can seldom go straight.

The HISTORY of St. Jean de Luz is too interesting to be wholly omitted.

After bravely resisting and checking the
Normans in the ninth century, it had already
become a flourishing town in the thirteenth
century, when whale-fishing was in its palmy
days.

Its proud inhabitants then enjoyed wonderful liberties, and their immunities were
confirmed by Louis XI., who spent a long
time there in 1463.

A pilot of St. Jean de Luz (Sanchez de
Huelva) is said to have first suggested to
Columbus the possible existence of America.
In any case, its sailors knew Iceland very well
as far back as 1412, and there is little doubt
about their having discovered Newfoundland
in the middle of the fifteenth century, many
years before the great discovery of Columbus.

Francis I. spent a few hours here after his
captivity.

The town was taken and burnt by the

Spaniards in 1558, and a few years after
(1565) it was visited by Charles IX. It was
towards the close of the same century that
500 persons were cruelly burnt to death for
sorcery. About the same period, whales gradually disappeared from the Bay of Biscay,
going to northern oceans,—a severe loss for
the almost exclusively "maritime" population
of these regions. Still, the manly sailors of
St. Jean de Luz, far from losing courage,
pursued the "monsters of the deep" as far
as the Spitzbergen seas, and also went to
Newfoundland for cod-fishing, in 200 and
300-ton ships. How times have changed!
How empty and silent its roadstead and long
streets now seem!

This doomed and unhappy town was re-
taken by the Spaniards in 1636, and the
Socoa fort was built in 1640, although the
present pier only dates from 1829.

But the greatest, or at least the most memo-
rable event connected with the history of St.
Jean de Luz, was the marriage of Louis XIV.
(June, 1660) with the Infanta of Spain, Maria-
Theresa, of Austria. The great monarch spent
six weeks in the town.

Then dawned the most prosperous days of

this now melancholy place. Under Colbert
(end of seventeenth century), it had eighty
first-class vessels, manned by 3000 magnificent
sailors. But hundreds of its brave children
fell at the naval disaster of La Hogue (1692).

With the wars of Louis XIV. began its
ruin, and it never ceased to decline since.
Misery and emigration first contributed to its
depopulation, calamities sadly aggravated
since that time by the resistless fury and invasion of the ocean, whose first serious advance took place in 1675. It was still worse
during the eighteenth century, when the
havoc became incredible. Nothing could
stand such waves, and the 22nd of January,
1749, was a memorable and fearful day, seven
houses being utterly destroyed, and 180 others
undermined, and abandoned in a few hours.
In 1782 another hurricane swept away all the
works of defence and two entire streets, besides
a convent of Ursulines, a part of the town
being quite submerged by the waves. It was
then that Louis XVI., to save St. Jean de Luz
from total destruction, began the granite pier
of *Ste. Barbe,* on the eastern side of the bay.
In three years nearly 500 feet of it had been

constructed, and the works resisted the waves
for half a century, but at last they also were
shattered to pieces, and the great breakwater,
now daily and majestically advancing on from
the *Socoa* fort eastward, is the only hope left
for St. Jean de Luz, where the sea is now
encroaching on the land at the rate of a yard
per annum, and threatening a dozen houses.
In fact, at very low water, heaps of ruins are
disclosed on the beach.

Napoleon I. visited St. Jean de Luz in 1808,
with gigantic ideas, which all came to nothing,
as politics gave him too much trouble, and left
him no time to battle with nature. It was in
1819 that the most serious attempts were made
to protect this town from its relentless foe, the
sea. A kind of "Chinese wall," no less than
50 feet wide, and 33 feet high, with three
ranges of huge piles running between it and
the sea, was raised like a regular fortification
along the side of St. Jean de Luz facing the
Atlantic. It was quite Cyclopean, and looked
invulnerable; but it was so completely destroyed in 1822 by a hurricane, which lasted
a whole week, that according to the report of
the engineers themselves, not a fragment of it

could be found after! 500 feet of the most formidable masonry were carried off like dust or feathers!

But happily, within the last few years, this fearful sea appears to be relatively calming down, and such paroxysms as those have not been known for fifty years. Besides, the Socoa breakwater is now steadily progressing; it is to be about 1100 feet long, and another is soon to be begun from the other or eastern side of the harbour, where the hill of *Ste. Barbe* projects its mournful ruins against the blue sky. These ruins (a short mile north of St. Jean de Luz) are those of a fort. The view of the Bay of Biscay from this point is superb. It is the same from Socoa, a village and fort standing on the other side, west of St. Jean de Luz (a mile and a half). You can drive to Socoa, and you should not omit to walk a little way to the left (west) of it, where the foam slides up and down the brilliant slopes of schist peculiar to this coast. On sunny days it is a beautiful sight.

To go to Socoa, you first cross the *Nivelle*, a small but pretty stream, which descends from the east of *La Rhune*, through a hilly and very green country: then you enter *Ciboure*, a suburb of St. Jean de Luz, with a large population of gipsies (*cascarotacs*), and a bathing establishment. The men are almost all sailors.

To drive to Socoa, you must now go a very long way round; the direct road along the sea being cut and out of repair. It is a shorter distance to walk than to drive.

The three things to be seen *in* St. Jean de Luz are : the *Church*, built by the English in the thirteenth or fourteenth century. It is in the main street. The *château* where the king spent six weeks, and that of his bride, the Infanta.

There is a good bathing establishment on the northern beach (half a mile), with a *buffet* and reading-room; but it is closed in November.

About 1500 strangers visit the place every summer, and Napoleon III. often came.

The natives are particularly peaceful and friendly, and they always were so : the most perfect security did not cease to exist even in the sanguinary times of the " Terreur." There were only two executions.

N.B.—There are fine fossils on the hill of Ste. Barbe (north side : *Fucoïdes*).

N.B.—The express train from Paris to Madrid, the one almost always taken to go to St. Jean de Luz, passes through the Biarritz station a little before one o'clock P.M. But no train returns till late in the evening.

CHAPTER IX.

HENDAYE, FUENTERRABIA, SAN SEBASTIAN.

IT is very easy to see these three places in one day from Biarritz, by taking the Paris and Madrid express train at one o'clock P.M. at the Biarritz station (two miles off), and returning by the evening train, which leaves San Sebastian between six and seven o'clock P.M., reaching Biarritz before ten o'clock P.M. By doing it thus you have an hour to spare at the *Irun* station (in Spain), which allows time enough to see *Fuenterrabia* (two miles from the Irun station) and return, so as to continue your journey in the Madrid express, leaving Irun at 2.30 (Spanish time). When you come back in the evening, the train stops another hour at *Hendaye* (towards eight o'clock P.M.), and there you can dine at the railway "table d'hôte."

But some people, to be more free of their motions, prefer driving the whole distance to San Sebastian and back, in all nearly 80

English miles. It is therefore impossible to
do it thus on the same day, except with a
change of horses at Irun or Hendaye. The
only advantage of driving is to leave you
ample time for visiting the strange, but very
small town of Fuenterrabia, which, let it be
remembered, is *not* on the railway, but two
miles exactly north of it. The railway route
will first be described.

As far as St. Jean de Luz, see preceding
chapter. You now travel west, through a
hilly country, with deep cuttings, which shut
out the view. You can just catch a glimpse
(south) of the *Urrugne* village and fields (see
below), with the wild mountain of *La Rhune*
behind (2920 feet); and beyond (six miles
from St. Jean de Luz) you get a passing sight,
on your right, of the proud Gothic castle
belonging to the great African explorer and
savant, M. Antoine d'Abbadie. But there is
no landscape to speak of till you enter the
valley of the *Bidassoa*, after passing a long
tunnel, and descend to *Hendaye*, the last station
in France (16 miles from the Biarritz station).

It is on the right bank of the *Bidassoa*, and
nearly due east of the Spanish town of *Fuen-*

terrabia, well seen on the other side, as the river, although not two miles from its mouth in the ocean, is but two-thirds of a mile across. At all tides, and with the most perfect security, you can go by boat from Hendaye to Fuenterrabia in the smoothest water, the awful surf beyond being quite broken by sandbanks, which look like fragments of a desert. Indeed, this is perhaps the shortest and the best of all ways to see Fuenterrabia without interrupting your journey to San Sebastian. But you would thus have to walk two miles from Fuenterrabia to the station of Irun, where your train stops an hour. It is only a few pence for crossing the *Bidassoa,* a poor but picturesque little river, which flows entirely through Spain for about 30 miles, nearly due north, and then for the last eight miles of its course divides it from France.

Hendaye is only a village of about 700 inhabitants, with a tolerable hotel (*International*), facing the Spanish hill of *Jaysquivel* (2200 feet), so well seen from Biarritz. In 1793 it was mercilessly bombarded at night by the Spaniards of Fuenterrabia, and without any warning. It was reduced to ashes, but

H

fifteen months after the latter town capitulated to 300 French soldiers.

Its liqueur is famous, and the "buffet" at the station not bad.

The scenery is indeed beautiful, though never grand: for wherever you look you see verdure or blue waters, backed by bold brown hills, the highest and most conspicuous of which is the *Haya* (3100 feet), called *Trois Couronnes* in France, here close by, to the south. Then every acre of the lowlands is dotted with Basque farm-houses, of dazzling whiteness. The sea appears in the distance, as blue as indigo, beyond the waving fields of maize.

The château of M. d'Abbadie, one of the finest in the south of France, and often called *Aragorria*, crowns a hill to the north-east of Hendaye, and three miles from it. The best way up to it is by the beach. After twelve years of travelling in the Ethiopian deserts, this eminent astronomer and linguist has now settled here, on a glorious Basque hill, between the Atlantic and the sky, devoting his life to his wife and science.

After passing Hendaye, the railway to

Madrid crosses the Bidassoa on a handsome bridge, and enters the Spanish province of *Guipuscoa.* On your left (south), high up on a rugged and brown hill, see the white chapel of *St. Martial,* where Marshal Soult, in 1813, unsuccessfully attacked the Spanish troops. (Pilgrimages every year.) *

. You now reach *Irun,* the first Spanish town, 18 miles from the Biarritz station, and lying at the foot of the serrated mountain of *Haya* (*Trois-Couronnes*), which rises in gentle slopes south of it (3100 feet), at a distance of three miles as the crow flies, but in reality of about five. Looked at from here, it has a great analogy of shape and of structure with the peak of *La Rhune,* seen from St. Jean de Luz; and its ascent is very much like the one of its neighbour and rival. In other words, it is by the north it is most easily climbed, its western sides being rather precipitous. By the north it is quite easy, and guides are useless. Going at first south from Irun, you soon turn a little to the left, and ascend the first spurs of the mountain, on a reddish soil dotted with chest-

---

* Since this was written, the Carlists have added a new celebrity to St. Martial.

nut-trees. Then crossing a ravine and a stream, and ascending to the right up a track in zigzags, you reach a bare plateau (just as on La Rhune), north of the ridge, very like a saw, which forms the top. An hour from here, steering south up easy slopes, takes you to the summit (two hours and a half from Irun). It is a long, narrow, and serrated arête, with a marvellous view of sea and mountains, and a great precipice to the west. You see much less of France but more of Spain than from La Rhune, which is also 200 feet lower. Seen from Biarritz, the *Haya* bears S.S.W.

This mountain, where foxes are common, is pierced with galleries and wells for the extraction of iron. Now all abandoned.

A good pedestrian, in a long summer day, can easily ascend the *Trois-Couronnes* from Biarritz, even by taking the one o'clock P.M. train, which will leave him five hours to dispose of at Irun. Driving from Biarritz makes it easier still.

At the Irun station you will always find omnibuses ready to take you either to the town itself (half a mile distant), or to Fuenterrabia. You have an hour to spare.

Here the railway time changes, Madrid time, of course, being adopted. It is twenty-five minutes behind Paris time, and this leaves you an hour's stoppage. No passports required.

You must change trains, as the fears of a French invasion have induced the Spaniards to adopt on their railway lines a gauge wider by a foot than that of their jealous and quarrelsome neighbours.

Besides a *buffet*, there is a large hotel (*de la Viscayna*) near the Irun station, and another in the town (*Arrupe*). The latter is well known to most British tourists.

Irun (in Basque "good place") has a population of nearly 6000 souls, and a rather heavy-looking, but fine church. Roman walls and medals were found in the neighbourhood.

To see *Fuenterrabia* (two miles north) hire an omnibus or a carriage at the Irun station. The hour you have to spare is quite sufficient. Splendid Indian-corn.

Fuenterrabia (in Basque *Ondarrabia*, "sandy river") is a most thoroughly Spanish town of 3000 inhabitants, with picturesque, but gloomy streets, a crowd of beggars, latticed windows, clouds of dust, and ruined battlements. Desolation is upon it everywhere. Silent and heavy, but pompous *palacios*, with monstrous escutcheons, still bear witness to its ancient splendour. See the church (Gothic inside) and the view from the terrace. See also the *castle*, built towards 907. The Basques are here strikingly handsome.

Battles without end have been fought here, and some walls are riddled with bullets. In 1638, a mutiny having broken out in the French army which besieged it, the garrison made a furious sortie, which cost the French more than 2000 men, mostly drowned in the Bidassoa. In the present century, Fuenterrabia was four times taken and re-taken (1808-1837).

From the light-house of Cape *Figuier* (two miles north of Fuenterrabia), 320 feet above the sea, you can see all the Bay of Biscay; and of course better still, if you ascend the lofty hill of *Jaysquivel*, a bare and breezy ridge, eight miles long, which extends towards the West as far as *Passages* (see below), rising in one place to 2200 feet out of the great Atlantic. If you do this, you will pass by the storm-beaten convent and church of *N. D. de Guadalupe*, so well seen on the hill west of

Fuenterrabia. It is fully three hours' walk over the ridge of Jaysquivel to Passages, and it is both pleasanter and safer always to follow the summit, as the slopes towards the sea are torn all the way by endless and countless ravines, which double the distance.

After this digression, we shall now resume our journey to San Sebastian.

Beyond Irun the line travels west, through a very pretty and fertile country, with bleak hills rising on either side. You soon leave *Renteria* on your left (seven miles from Irun), and then, on your right, the beautiful and almost land-locked little port of *Pasajes*, with bold headlands frowning at its mouth. Here Lafayette sailed for America.

Fantastical villas of every style, scattered everywhere, now give you signs of wealth and civilization as you approach

San Sebastian, a modern and geometrical city of 16,000 inhabitants (17 miles from Irun, 37 from Biarritz). It is the capital of the Basque province of Guipuzcoa,

Omnibuses at the station, which is half a mile from the town. You pass a splendid bridge.

Hotels: *de Inglaterra (Beraza), de Londres, Royal Hôtel, &c., &c.*

The general aspect is rather Parisian than Spanish; the streets are very clean and straight. The town stands on a peninsula, on the south-eastern side of a massive and strongly-fortified hill (*Orgullo*); it is one of the most frequented sea-bathing places in Spain.

See the church of Santa Maria, five minutes' walk from the hotels.

Very good shops, and excellent cigars at *de la Houssaye's, Calle de la Alameda*, 27. You can take back to France, free of duty, as many as will fill your pockets. If it rains, take shelter in the fine *Café de la Marina*, on the *Alameda*, where the garrison band plays on summer evenings, before a procession of lovely Basque women.

But on a fine day you should walk up the hill of *Orgullo*, whose citadel seems to threaten the Atlantic from a height of 375 feet. The view is grand, though the Biarritz coast is hidden by a bold headland. You can ascend the hill on either side, and walk all round it, observing, as you pass its western side, the dilapidated graves of many a British officer. Assaulted and taken in 1813 by the Duke of Wellington, San Sebastian was sacked, and then set on fire. "Facts," says Henry O'Shea in his remarkable *Guide to Spain*, "must not be disfigured to please patriotism, and this is one of the very few black spots on the glorious sun of England." . . . The British loss in this assault amounted to 5000 killed and wounded.

San Sebastian has bull-fights, a theatre, a casino, and there is much gambling.

With a few hours to spend there, you should hire a boat, cross the harbour from east to west, and ascend the pyramidal hill which rises west of San Sebastian to a height of about 500 feet above the sea-level. From the old tower on the summit you can well see Biarritz and its lofty light-house, and the long sandy beach fading away in the extreme north-east towards Arcachon.

The harbour of San Sebastian is unsafe and shallow. The fish is excellent.

To return the same evening to Biarritz, you can either dine at the table d'hôte of one of the hotels at six o'clock, or at the *buffet* of Hendaye at eight o'clock, as the train from

Spain stops an hour there. You reach Biarritz at ten o'clock P.M.

Should you wish to drive all the way from Biarritz to San Sebastian, better sleep in the latter place, to avoid a drive of almost 80 miles on the same day. The high road not following the railway line, will now be described.

Leaving Biarritz by the road which leads to the railway station, you meet, just before this station, the majestic but formal road from Paris to Madrid. Take it (right). Four miles from Biarritz will place you on the hill of *Bidart*, a gay village, where you enter the Basque country. Then you descend, and climbing another hill, you soon reach *Guétharry*, with its milk-white Basque houses, two small hotels, a modest sea-bathing establishment, and a sandy little harbour. Fine sea-view.

(It is five miles by the beach from Biarritz to Guétharry, a weary walk along the sands. Ophite and strange fossils are found in the rocks. You have to cross two streams.)

After Guétharry the road is perfectly straight for four miles, but *La Rhune* and other mountains are always in sight.

St. Jean de Luz is ten miles from Biarritz

(see Chap. VIII.). Follow the road to Spain.
Two miles farther you pass close to *Urtubie*, a
" modernized " old manor, belonging to the
De Larralde family. Wellington and other
great men slept there. Hilly country. A
very short mile beyond you cross the village
of *Urrugne*, with a sad inscription on the
clock of its church, meaning, " *They all
wound; the last one kills.*" You then ascend
a hill, carried by the Allies in 1813, and with
a splendid view of sea and mountains. In
1793 there was also severe fighting here.
Ruins of redoubts.

Leaving on the right the railway and *Hendaye* (see above), you descend towards the
west, facing the glorious hills of Spain, where
the *Haya*, or "*Trois-Couronnes*," overtops all
others. (South; see above.)

At length you come to *Béhobie*, the last
town in France (17 miles from Biarritz), with
two hotels, and on the right bank of the
Bidassoa, which separates the two kingdoms.
Half of the bridge belongs to France, and
the other to Spain.

On the right is the celebrated but insignificant island, *des Faisans*, where, in 1659, the marriage settlements of Louis XIV. were signed by Cardinal Mazarin and Don Luis de Haro. A little pyramid stands on it.

Two miles from Béhobie take you, through a swampy but well-cultivated country, to *Irun,* where you join the railway route described above. And beyond Irun the road always follows the same tract of country as the railway line, the distances being nearly the same (37 miles both ways from Biarritz to San Sebastian).

CHAPTER X.

DAX, BUGLOSE, AND THE LANDES.

DAX is a small town of not quite 10,000 inhabitants, 31 miles (by rail) north-east of Bayonne, on the river Adour, and just an hour from Bayonne by rail. It was well known to the Romans, and called by Cæsar *Aquæ* (waters); hence "Dax." Its old ramparts are certainly of Roman origin.

Hotels: de l'Europe, and de France. Omnibuses at the station.

Bull-ring and cathedral. But the celebrity of Dax is due to its waters, and its mud-baths. One of the springs, remarkable for its abundance as well as for its temperature (158° Fahr.), is constantly covered with clouds of vapour, like the boiling mouth of a small volcano. In general, the Dax waters are used for rheumatism, especially in spring.

A very rich rock-salt mine, near the town, became three or four years ago the property

of a celebrated English " savant," Mr. Max-
well-Lyte.

All the environs of Dax are full of thermal
springs.

Roman mosaics and aqueducts have also
been found quite near the town, and in it.

Steamers have ceased to run on the charming river Adour.

Buglose is a village, five miles north of Dax,
but not on the Paris road. A station has that
name on the Bordeaux and Dax Railway ; but
it is a mile and a half from the famous monastery. Some trains, however, at certain times
of the year, stop at Buglose itself, where there
are several little inns.

A Catholic need not be told what gives such
interest to this otherwise unknown little village, lost in a wilderness of silent pine-forests
and sand. It was within a few miles of it (at
Pouey) that St. Vincent de Paul was born in
1576, and miracles beyond dispute have more
than once hallowed the soil of Buglose.

Buglose is only five miles from Dax, where
you can get any number of vehicles to carry
you to it. Taking the Paris road for two and
a half miles without any objects of interest, you

then leave it and turn to the left, where you behold the cupola of the *Pouey* church, whose altar stands on the spot where St..Vincent de Paul was born. This beautiful building is well seen from the train as you go to Paris (right-hand side), at two miles after the Dax station. There is a Lazarist convent at Pouey, and opposite the church stands the majestic oak under which the great Saint, nearly 300 years ago, meditated in his boyhood. There is also a school, and a large hospital for old and invalid persons. Relics are shown of St. Vincent, who died in Paris in 1660.

From Pouey, the Buglose road goes nearly three miles through a gloomy pine-forest. And here I cannot do better than quote Mr. Shyne Lawlor (' *Pilgrimages in the Pyrenees and Landes* '), in whose poetical pages heart and intellect always go together.

"On the confines of the Landes and Chalosse, in the parish illustrated by the birth of St. Vincent de Paul, and in the middle of the sands, stands an ancient shrine, venerable in the traditions of the country and the faith of its inhabitants. Countless pilgrims have knelt before it in bygone times, and their number

has not diminished in the present day. Few
spots are more favourable to meditation and
prayer. The only noise that intrudes upon
the peaceful retreat is that of the tread of
pilgrims, the song of psalmody, the lowing of
the herds, or that melancholy and indefinable
harmony which the pine-forest sends forth as
it replies to the breeze. To the north and
east of the chapel, plains of sand, covered by
a low heather, spread to an unlimited extent:
to the west are visible the vast forests of Ma-
rensin: in the distant south, the horizon is
bounded by the rugged peaks of the Pyrenees,
and by the fertile hills of Chalosse, watered by
the winding Adour. On one side nature is
all severe—arid sand, solitary steppes: on the
other, she reigns over graceful sites, pleasant
valleys, and grassy fields. Above this varied
landscape towers Our Lady of Buglose, invok-
ing upon it the blessing and protection of
Heaven." (*'Pilgrimages,'* &c., page 567.)

The origin of the Buglose pilgrimages is
uncertain; but centuries ago they already
took place. See the lovely statue of the
Blessed Virgin, seated on a throne of marble.
The graceful attitude, harmonious proportions

and tender expression of this admirable statue all combine to render it a masterpiece, due probably to the early period of the Renaissance. In all fairness however, it must be admitted that the present statue has not been proved to be the same as the one which rendered Buglose famous, before even the Huguenot wars. (See Lawlor, pages 569 and 570.)

The Oratory having been sacked in 1570, by order of Jeanne d'Albret, the Catholics concealed their dear statue in a morass, where it lay fifty years, and was at last found again by shepherds, or rather by one of their oxen; hence *Buglose* (Greek *Bous,* "an ox," and *glossa,* "tongue").

The present church is very grand indeed (Romanesque style). The pilgrimages take place on Pentecost Mondays. Here also Lazarists are found, and an asylum for aged and infirm priests. In 1856, there was a superb gathering, numbering no less than 600 priests; and in 1866 also, for the coronation of the statue.

Several trains stop daily at the Buglose station (one mile and a half distant); but when pilgrimages take place, and in the month of May, they stop at the monastery itself.

There is a strange and solemn harmony between the shrine of Buglose and the *Landes* scenery. The Landes are, on the whole, an awful wilderness, where a hundred miles can be travelled in a given line, on white sand forming great waves, and through endless pine-forests, mixed with cork-trees, twisted like demons. Except the wind, and the roar of the sea, nothing is ever heard in those deserts, though here and there you meet shepherds walking on stilts; they can thus go seven miles an hour. It is an unhealthy and swampy land, with dismal lakes, which become seas after the autumn rains; pines and poplar-trees emerge everywhere from the waste of waters, where hills form islands. For weeks after a flood, travelling in some parts of the Landes is all by water. In summer the white sand reverberates an Indian heat; and even then the soil is often treacherous, for there are pools beneath, where you sink through the sand.

The inhabitants are far too badly fed to be anything but wretched; the water is impure, the land swampy, and the best thing they eat is maize.

Still the Landes are a rich country, thanks to the tar, or essence of turpentine (*résine*), extracted from those millions of pines. But the tree must be at least fifteen years old before it can produce it. Immense fortunes were made in this apparently useless country, during the American war; and some land-lords own whole territories, worth 10,000*l.* a year, or even more. Their greatest enemy is *fire;* there are fearful conflagrations. Besides, sandstorms in the Landes are a serious affair; they amount to a real danger, though the sand-hills (*Dunes*) are nearly stopped now by the plantation of the pine, whose roots harden and fix the sand. But a few years ago, the sea used to encroach on this unhappy coast at the rate of from 60 to 70 feet a year! the sand-hills moving on towards the east like waves.

It is indeed a strange country, unlike any other part of Europe, and well worth a visit.

CHAPTER XI.

CAP-BRETON.

CAP-BRETON (*Caput Bruti*) is a village of 1300 inhabitants, in the Landes, 13 miles north of Bayonne, and rather more than a mile from the ocean. It is in a very swampy, although sandy country, mostly covered with great pines.

Better drive all the way from Biarritz (18 miles), unless you take the early morning train from Bayonne to Bordeaux, as far as the *Labenne* station, only four miles from Cap-Breton, where, in this case, you must remain till the evening.

Taking the Paris road, north of Bayonne, you first go through a populous and well-cultivated country, with gay villas, gardens, and fields on both sides, speaking of wealth, comfort, and civilization. But beyond the village of *Tarnos* (three miles from Bayonne), culture and civilization both disappear, the wilderness begins: pines and twisted cork-trees replace poplars and oaks, and you enter the almost boundless solitudes of the *Landes* (Chap. X.) where the sea-breeze howls night and day through the lofty pines. Here and there, however, the depressing monotony of the landscape is still broken by small tarns, as motionless as the Dead Sea, whilst in the extreme distance (S.E.) you get glimpses of snowy peaks.

Labenne (8½ miles from Bayonne; 13½ from Biarritz) is a station on the Bordeaux railway line. There used to be a lake (*Orx*) to the east of it, covering thousands of acres till a few years ago: but the whole place was drained, and not a trace of it is left.

After crossing the village of Labenne (half a mile beyond the station), and admiring its pretty church, you leave the Paris road to your right, and go due north towards Cap-Breton, on a much less formal and narrow road, between sand-hills of every size and shape, looking like huge waves. The sand is almost snow-white, and throws out an intense heat in summer. Still, some verdure is left, in the shape of ferns and pines. *Cistus* is abundant. Not a house is seen for four miles, till you reach

Cap-Breton, one mile from the sea, and on a sort of stream (the Boudigau), in colour more like beer than water. Little boats ascend it with the tide. You can breakfast at the Hôtel *Marin*.

This village was once very important, when the capricious river Adour here fell into the sea. But a fearful storm, 300 years ago, having swollen the Pyrenæan torrents to such an extent that they almost deluged all the Bayonne country, this irresistible irruption of waters again opened the natural basin of the Adour, by forcing the sand on both sides, and it left Cap-Breton for Bayonne. But before that, its bed had changed many times, and this restless river most probably ran into the ocean at Cap-Breton in the thirteenth century; later it went still farther north. By this now almost empty village one hundred ships were once anchored.

By crossing the Boudigau, and walking west for one mile over vine-covered sand-hills (producing the well-known *vin de sable*), you reach the Atlantic, under whose blue waters opens the gulf, or submarine valley called *Fosse de Cap-Breton*. Whilst on both sides of this deep gorge there is shallow water everywhere, the soundings give 200 fathoms over the *Fosse*, at less than a mile from land. It is supposed to run from east to west under the Atlantic for about seven miles, its width being from two to three. The sea is quite smooth over the *Fosse*, even when it boils on both sides of it. Still, it is full of currents.

Due north of Cap-Breton, two short miles distant, see the strange lake *Hossgort*. The sand, silence, and pines which surround this blue sheet of water (a mile and a half long), remind you so vividly of Australia or Canada, that you cannot realize you are still in Europe. (Do not get lost in the pine-forests upon the right of the lake.)

From Cap-Breton to Dax, 27 miles: good carriage-road.

LAC D'YRIEU.

A charming and easy excursion from Biarritz. You can drive the whole distance (14 miles). Go to Bayonne (five miles), and take the Paris road, as in the preceding section. At about 200 yards before the railway crossing, near the *Labenne* station, you turn off to the right, in your carriage, plunging into a grand pine-forest. A mile over sand takes you to Lake d'*Yrieu* (14 miles from Biarritz). The nearest village to it is *Ondres* (two short miles). There are dense woods round the lake, whose undulating banks rise in some places to about 100 feet, all covered with "jungle," and on whose still waters foliage everywhere droops in graceful festoons. It seems asleep in a cradle of leaves and flowers. The Pyrenees stand out clear in the distance (80 miles, and more). Observe, to the south-east, the proud fork of the *Pic du Midi de Pau* (9793 feet).

In the heat of summer, there is no better place for picnicking.

CHAPTER XII.

SARE AND ITS CAVES.

Sare is a large village, to the east of *La Rhune* (see Chap. XIII.), and almost due south of Biarritz, distant 18 miles by the woods of *Othecara*, and three miles less by *Arbonne;* but the latter road is detestable for carriages, the former very good.

After crossing the Biarritz railway station, you ascend a rugged and steep hill to the east, and then, leaving on your right (south) the Arbonne road, very bad for carriages, you continue for two miles to the east. The conical and conspicuous mountain which rises in the south-east, to the height of more than 6000 feet, is the *Orrhy*, the highest of the Basque hills (see Chap. XVI.); it is 45 miles distant.

At four and a half miles from Biarritz you must turn sharply to the south (right), and passing the château and village of *Arcangues*, from whence is a beautiful view of the Basque

plains and Pyrenees, you soon enter a wilder
and most hilly country, where the road,
ascending, descending, and always winding,
nearly doubles the actual distance. In fact, the
whole distance between Biarritz and Sare is,
as the crow flies, only 11 miles, although you
have to go 18. When you are about nine miles
from Biarritz, all traces of culture disappear,
not a house is in sight, and you enter the
great wood of St. Pée for three miles, going
up and down, and in endless semicircles, between small oaks and gorse, whose yellow
tints redeem the ugliness of the barren and
brown moors stretching between the trees.

At 12 miles from Biarritz you fall into the
Arbonne road, mentioned above, and three
miles shorter, and, emerging from the forest,
you descend (south-west) a long hill facing
the La Rhune mountain (2920 feet). The
village of St. Pée now appears below, with the
fields bordering the *Nivelle*.

St. Pée (2600 inhabitants; several inns) is
14 miles from Biarritz (11 by Arbonne), 13
from Bayonne, 8 from St. Jean de Luz, 7 from
Espelette (Chap. VII.), and rather more than
4 from Sare.

St. Pée has many old and picturesque Basque houses, and a good church.

To go to Sare, you start south, cross the *Nivelle* (which falls into the sea at St. Jean de Luz), and then gradually turn round towards the south-west, through a hilly and very green country, with the massive *La Rhune* straight before you.

You scarcely know when you enter *Sare,* so widely scattered are all its houses. It contains between 2000 and 3000 inhabitants. There is a comfortable inn, or small hotel, in the same building as the *Mairie.* There also you are sure to find a guide and candles, to visit the Sare caves, of which there are at least three very fine ones, the best of all being the one visited, in 1858, by Napoleon III. and the Empress, and opening south of Sare (four long miles), under the northern, or French side of the *Pic Atchuria* (2500 feet).

The church of Sare is both large and pretty, like most of the Basque churches.

To go to the grotto of Atchuria, or of *Lesia,* take a boy and candles, and give him 50 sous. You can drive two miles towards the grotto, and ride the whole way. There are ponies at

Sare. You go south, and after two miles,
leaving the high road, you have only to follow
up *ad libitum*, but always going up and down,
the right bank (left side) of a stream which is
one of the many sources of the Nivelle, and
issues from the cave of Lesia itself. The
country is dismal, but the Basque hills south
of you form a noble line, although almost
treeless. Four long miles from Sare take you
to the gloomy mouth of the *Lesia* grotto, forming a regular and splendid arch, at least 40
feet in height, and running far away, as level
as a floor, into the unknown depths of the
Atchuria peak, on the summit of which is the
Spanish frontier. In entering the cave, observe on the right an oval slab, commemo-
rating the Imperial visit of 1858; and on the
left, at a certain height, a mass of maiden-hair
fern, looking lovelier still with such darkness
near it.

There are numbers of other openings on
the sides and *over* the main cave, which is
composed of two stories, communicating with
each other by steep and muddy "couloirs,"
where a few steps are cut to help ladies. But
if once lost, even with a candle, in this mys-

terious maze, or system of grottoes running towards every point of the compass, and containing very deep pools, there would be little chance of escape. It is one of the most wonderful and one of the largest caves in the Pyrenees.

A clear streamlet gushes out of it, forming one of the numerous sources of the Nivelle. Bullock-carts have travelled a great way under the lofty vaults of the Lesia grotto, which is not half explored as yet.

The gloomy little village whose church is well seen to the east, in the middle of hills and moors, is *Zugarramurdy;* it is in Spain, though on the northern side of the Pyrenees, and on the banks of a river which enters France immediately. Here, as in many other places, the *natural* boundary (division of waters) has been sacrificed, in favour of Spain, to political considerations. But Zugarramurdy is too dirty to inspire any jealousy.

There are countless caves in this region. One to the east of the Lesia one, and only ten minutes' walk from it, with a very narrow opening, is very grand indeed. Further still to the east, and near *Urdax*, in Spain, there is a third, with a torrent running through it, and plenty of stalactites.

About three miles east of Zugarramurdy lies *Urdax* (in Spain also), with a few trees, and what was once a monastery. Gloomy church.

West of the Lesia cave, and on a *col* between the peaks of *Atchuria* and *Ibantelly*, see a line of lofty trees. Here are the *Palombières* of Sare. Huge nets are stretched in the autumn between these trees to catch ringdoves, in their annual flight from the north, across the Pyrenees. They never come with a westerly wind. (For more details, see Germond de Lavigne's '*Biarritz.*') It is a pretty walk of four miles from Sare; there are a few *cabanes*, or inns, near the summit.

N.B.— Five short miles east of Sare, and on the right bank of the Nivelle, is the village of *Ainhoa*, the last in France, on the Bayonne and Pamplona road. Inn, *Opoka*. It is situated on a well-cultivated and healthy plateau, between 400 and 500 feet above the sea-level, and west of the *Mondarrain* peak (Chap. VII.). Pilgrimages on Whit Monday. Ruins of a redoubt;

curious church. Grand view towards the
N.W., from the top of the hill on whose
slopes the chapel stands. The Atlantic is in
sight, and the Biarritz light-house, &c. Fine
place for sketching, though there is little
shade; chestnut-trees here and there. The
Spanish frontier is only two short miles south
of Ainhoa, at the junction of two torrents
which are the real source of the Nivelle.
Ainhoa is 17 miles from Bayonne; excellent
road.

From Sare you can drive back to Biarritz
by Ascain (N.W.) and St. Jean de Luz, the
distance being nearly the same (19 miles).
It is five miles from Sare to Ascain, over a
wild *col* about 1400 feet above the sea-level,
and N.E. of *La Rhune,* of which you never
lose sight. The road is both narrow and bad,
but never dangerous; slopes gentle.

From Ascain to St. Jean de Luz it is four
long miles, by the right bank of the Nivelle;
10 miles more take you back to Biarritz (see
Chap. VIII.).

A wretched diligence, like an old and
broken box, leaves Bayonne for Sare three
times a week, in the afternoon, starting from

the "Hôtel des Pyrénées," south of the town, in a dark street falling into the Rue d'Espagne.

It was by the side facing Sare that the allied armies under Wellington attacked and took *La Rhune* in October, 1813, with a loss of 1600 men. (See Napier, book xxii.)

For the fighting on the Nivelle, see Napier, book xxiii., chap. i.

CHAPTER XIII.

ASCENT OF LA RHUNE (2920 FEET).

IT is very easy to do this in one day from
Biarritz; and any one after spending an hour
in it, is sure to know La Rhune by sight:
what Mont Blanc is to Chamounix, La Rhune
is to Biarritz. It rises nobly, a few degrees
west of south, at a distance (mathematically
speaking) of 11 miles; but in reality, from
Biarritz to the top you have to go 18 miles,
of which you can drive 14 if you ascend by
Ascain (north of La Rhune), or else 18 if you
go by *Sare* (see preceding chapter), which is
due east of it. Better go up one way and
down the other, sending on your carriage
from one village to the other. The ascent
by Sare is longer, but less steep. Both at
Sare and Ascain there are inns for breakfast,
and generally ponies for ladies who prefer
ascending on horseback; but sometimes none
are to be found.

If you ascend by Ascain, leave Biarritz to-

K

wards eight o'clock A.M., and drive to *St. Jean
de Luz* (10 miles; see Chap. VIII.), whence
you can either go by boat up the Nivelle with
the tide to Ascain, or drive to it by the right
bank, always facing La Rhune, which forms
an imposing mass. The country is charming,
Indian-corn, meadows, and woods alternating
with rugged little cliffs, quite yellow with
gorse.

It is a little over 14 miles from Biarritz to
Ascain, where you can get guides (5 fr.) if
you want them, and breakfast at the inn *De la
Rhune*, near the church. Do not leave Ascain
later than 12 o'clock.

Two hours from here will take a *man* to the
summit; but a lady takes three. There is not
the slightest difficulty anywhere, and you cannot even get lost (save in a mist) on these
absolutely bare slopes, where scarcely anything grows but ferns; although La Rhune
was once covered with woods, which were
either burnt, or cut down for ship-building.
It is now bald as a skull.

Seen from Ascain, a great ravine, generally
dry, seems to split it in two for half of its
height; and by far the shortest way to the

summit is up the left bank (right side as you go up) of this rocky gutter. But it is easier to leave this on your left, and ascend S.S.W., instead of due south. The slopes are much gentler, since bullock-carts ascend half of La Rhune by the blood-red road you see winding up to the right of the *Huaïtz* torrent, under the doubtful shadow of stunted little oaks.

An hour's good walking takes you to a solitary house, with seven oaks to the right (or west) of it; and here you reach an undulating and shadeless plateau, covered with ferns and furze. After passing a few "cabanes," you go straight to the peak, rising abruptly before you, due south, and without a tree. Very gentle zigzags, good enough for ponies, will easily lead you to the summit.

If you go by *Sare* (18 miles from Biarritz; see Chap. XII.), you can ascend on foot, and steering west, by the hideous gorge which on its eastern side also tears La Rhune in two parts. But on horseback you must follow a track, well seen from Sare, which ascends W.N.W., on the northern slope of the smaller of the two ridges (the right one) which here

E 2

descend from the summit. There is a most
conspicuous little house (well in sight of Sare)
which you must pass. After two hours of
monotonous climbing, you fall into the Ascain
track, on the plateau described above. On
the whole, the ascent of La Rhune is gentler
by Sare, but half an hour longer than by
Ascain.

The view from this summit (2920 feet) may
without hesitation be called one of the most
magnificent in Europe, combining a huge extent of sea and plains, with an almost endless
line of peaks.

All the Bay of Biscay is there under your
feet, as on a map, from the Arcachon sands to
beyond Bilbao : in clear weather it is as blue
as the Mexican Sea, and the absence of ships
makes it look infinite. To the north-east, the
emerald-green plains of the Adour, glittering
with rivers, and dotted all over with villas, or
populous and snow-white Basque villages,
carry the spectator's eye or imagination to the
distant and still richer valley of the Garonne.
Far away to the east, the central Pyrenees
whiten the sky with their snows, and the
Pic du Midi de Bigorre, through 90 miles of

space, appears as plain as possible. South-east and south of La Rhune, it is a strange chaos of barren mountains, sun-burnt and almost repulsive; but dear to the poet or historian, by their memories, and the noble or cruel deeds they have been witnessing for such numbers of centuries, since Charlemagne first rendered them famous. An Englishman ought to carry Napier's 'Peninsula War' to the top of La Rhune, which was taken by its eastern side (October 1813), after hard fighting, and with a loss to the Allies of 1600 men. Ruins of a redoubt are still seen on the summit, where you also find traces of a chapel and "Hermitage," which was a school for the Sare boys before 1793. They used to spend a week up there.

A modern and ugly obelisk commemorates the late Emperor's ascent. Woodcocks and partridges are common on La Rhune, and the ferns are beautiful. The rocks are pudding-stone and red sandstone, and coal has been found.

On the slopes of La Rhune, vestiges still exist of a camp, called "Camp de la *Baïon-nette,*" where it is said the bayonet was first

used by the Basque soldiers in one of their
battles with the Spaniards; having run short
of cartridges, they fastened their formidable
knives to the muzzle of their guns, thus
inventing the bayonet.

PART II.

EXCURSIONS REQUIRING SEVERAL DAYS.

CHAPTER XIV.

GROTTO OF ISTURITZ.

It is 30 miles from Biarritz to Isturitz, by Cambo and Hasparren (see below); a little less by Bayonne and Hasparren (27 miles); in either case you had better sleep out one night, either at Cambo or at Hasparren. You can drive both ways.

The village of Isturitz is two miles to the north of the Bayonne and St. Palais road. Leaving Bayonne in a south-easterly direction, between the Nive and the Adour, you pass *St. Pierre d'Irube* (one mile and a half), beyond which you enter the Basque country, and a very hilly region, where woods now and then alternate with great moors. This is the road to *St. Palais.*

Hasparren or *Hasparr*, is a Basque town of

more than 5000 inhabitants, and containing a
whole population of shoemakers. Great cattle
markets. Over the main gate of the church
observe a marble slab with four Latin verses,
of which the meaning is much discussed.
This Roman inscription dates from Adrian (?),
A.D. 117. Fertile hills, rising to about 500 feet,
almost encircle Hasparren. It is exactly 15
miles from Bayonne, and consequently 20 from
Biarritz.

Following up the road to St. Palais, through
Bonloc, for about five miles beyond Hasparren,
you then leave it and turn to the left (north),
on a by-road, where you soon discover a half-
ruined tower on the top of a hill. Under this
tower runs the celebrated grotto of Isturitz,
through granite and limestone. It divides
into many branches, and forms a regular chaos
of rocks, with quantities of beautiful stalactites.
Under the cave runs the torrent of Arberoue,
which reappears at the surface a little farther
north, near the village of Isturitz. In certain
floods the torrent rises to the level of the
grotto and flows through it.

The hill of Isturitz is pierced with caves,
like a honeycomb.

Should you prefer going by Cambo, you had better sleep there; in which case the second day's drive will represent about 40 miles.

From Cambo to Hasparren it is seven miles, through a hilly and very rich country. At Hasparren continue as above.

From Hasparren to *St. Palais* it is 18 miles, over hills and moors. (See Chap. XVI.)

St. Palais is consequently 38 miles from Biarritz, passing through Hasparren.

LOYOLA.

1st. By Zumarraga.

Take the Madrid express (which passes the Biarritz station at about one o'clock P.M.) as far as San Sebastian, where you arrive at three o'clock. (See Chap. IX.)

The line beyond this becomes a piece of wonderful engineering, an endless succession of tunnels and bridges, especially of the former. It is a long, continual rise along the banks of the rapid *Oria*. The first town of importance is *Tolosa* (8000 inhabitants), a clean, well-built and busy Basque town, 47 miles from

Biarritz. Hôtel de las Diligencias. It is in a
charming valley, near the junction of two
rivers, the Azpiros and the Oria. Church of
Santa Maria. Over its portico there is a
colossal statue of St. John the Baptist.

Beyond Tolosa the line goes through four
tunnels, and crosses the Oria no less than
fifteen times in nine miles! After *Beasain*
(56 miles from Biarritz) there are nine tunnels
in succession and four crossings of the Oria,
besides a superb iron viaduct, 1000 feet long,
over the fertile valley of *Ormaïsteguy*. The
four stone piers supporting it are 120 feet
high. Again you cross six more tunnels
before reaching Zumarraga! In all, between
Irun and Zumarraga, there are nineteen
tunnels in 45 miles, and a rise of nearly
1200 feet. Still, this is as nothing compared
to the line beyond (towards Madrid), which
has to go through fourteen more tunnels
before reaching its greatest altitude (2000 feet)
on the Cantabrian Pyrenees!

Zumarraga is a village of 1400 inhabitants,
standing at an elevation of nearly 1200 feet,
on the banks of the river *Urola*, flowing north,
and separating it from *Villareal* (1000 inhabi-

tants). It is 65 miles from Biarritz, and the
one o'clock express from Paris arrives here at
4.40 P.M. At 5.30 a diligence leaves for
Azcoïtia (eight miles, 1s. 8d.); take it, leaving
the Madrid line. After crossing the Urola on a
stone bridge, you go through a hilly country,
on a good road, running northward, along the
waving banks of the river. Eight short miles
will thus take you to *Azcoïtia* (5000 inhabitants), on the left bank, in a wooded little
valley, and at the foot of the *Izarraiz*. There
is a 'fine church and an hotel. One mile,
across fields and gardens, takes you to
Loyola.

2nd. By Zaraus.

Leave the Biarritz station, either by the
early morning train, reaching San Sebastian
at 8.10 A.M., or else by the 1 o'clock P.M. express, reaching San Sebastian at 3 o'clock P.M.
Two diligences leave San Sebastian daily for
Zaraus, one at 11 o'clock A.M., the other at
3.30 P.M. The distance is sixteen miles; time,
two hours and a half; price, five shillings.
Better hire a carriage.

You leave San Sebastian, going westward,
through a charming and fertile country, where

you follow the coast. Eight miles take you to *Usurbil*, on a hill; fine church.

Then the road is often cut out of the solid rock, before *Orio*, where you cross the Oria on a fine bridge. Hilly country. Sixteen miles from San Sebastian, the traveller reaches

Zaraus (1300 inhabitants), a beautiful sea-bathing place, with a grand sandy beach, a healthy climate, handsome villas, and pretty hills with chestnut-trees. Hotel *Atristayne*.

Here cross a ridge (S.W.), and then descend into the *Urola* valley, with villages on both sides.

Santa Cruz de Cestona is a large village, one mile from the baths of *Cestona*, where there is a very good hotel (eight miles from Zaraus). Waters good for rheumatism. Boats on the Urola, and mules for mountain explorations. Better sleep here.

Azpeitia (13 miles from Zaraus) contains upwards of 5000 inhabitants. Posada Nueva. A wall surrounds it; see in the church the silver statuette of St. Ignatius de Loyola.

A mile beyond it (30 miles from San Sebastian) is the *Santa Casa* and convent where this great saint, the founder of the Jesuits, was born in 1491. You have green hills and woods all round you, and the clear Urola looks asleep as it winds across the lovely vale of *Iraurgui.*

The *church* of Loyola, one of the richest and handsomest in Spain, was built by the Roman architect, Fontana. Its proportions and symmetry are beautiful. The cupola (70 feet in diameter) is built of the peculiar granite called *ophite*, found in abundance in the neighbouring hills. The portico is adorned with black and highly-polished marble, jasper columns, grand lions, &c. Above the main entrance, observe a white statue of St. Ignatius. Once inside the church, gloomy marbles, alternating with red and white ones, almost make you shudder, as if night were rushing upon you; the altars are splendid, and wherever you look you see marble, alabaster, jasper, &c.

There are two towers each, 125 feet high, and the total height of the dome, cross included, is 166 feet. All the lines of this remarkable building are of exquisite grace.

An *hotel* stands near the monastery, which was built in 1683.

The church was not yet finished, when the Jesuits had to leave Spain, under Charles III.

There is a great pilgrimage yearly to Loyola (July 31st). Dancing and bull-fights, &c.

Biarritz to Loyola and back takes two short days, and you have thus the choice of two ways; but the best plan is to hire a carriage at San Sebastian.

CHAPTER XV.

BILBAO.

1st. Along the Coast.

Go by rail to San Sebastian (Chap. IX.), whence to Bilbao, by Guernica, 85 miles. It is a diligence road, but badly kept, especially near Bilbao.

As far as *Zaraus*, see Chap. XIV. (16 miles from San Sebastian). From here two and a half miles take you to *Guetairia*, a small harbour, with a Gothic church. After three more miles you reach the Urola, which you cross in a boat, and come to

Zumaya (1700 inhabitants), an old but very clean town (Roman). Sea-bathing place. You now go due west, along a hilly coast, and reach

Deva (29 miles from San Sebastian), a pretty town, as large as Biarritz, and very full in summer. It stands between the sea and high hills. Cross the Deva by boat.

Motrico (two miles from Deva) is famous

for its fish and vineyards. Here the hills are wooded. Two long miles from Motrico, out of sight of the sea, take you to

Ondarroa (33 miles from San Sebastian), at the end of an almost land-locked little bay, with wooded hills (chestnuts and oaks) on all sides. Iron mines. Road very bad.

Lequeitio (39 miles from San Sebastian) is a fortified town, with a beautiful view. From the top of the hill called *Alto de Lequeitio*, Biarritz is in sight (distance, 45 miles). There is a fine bridge, of one very bold arch. (2500 inhabitants.)

Now the road strikes inland (S.W.), through a very hilly country, for about 15 miles, to

Guernica (54 miles from San Sebastian), a Basque village, "where," says Murray in his 'Guide to Spain,' "was held the Parliament of Basque Senators. . . . . . This congress originally sat under the overspreading canopy of an ancient *oak*, which the town still bears on its shield. . . . . . The French republicans cut down, in 1808, the time-honoured oak of the free Basques, a tree which was very old even in 1334!"

Thirty-one more miles over a fertile, and

here and there wooded, but rough country, take you by *Mundaca, Bermes, Munguia,* and at last *Begoña,* to BILBAO (85 miles from San Sebastian).

2nd. By the Loyola Valley.

As far as *Azpeitia* (29 miles from San Sebastian), see Chap. XIV. Two miles farther south is *Ascoitia* (see Chap. XIV.), on the wooded banks of the Urola. Ascend (N.W.) the *Azcarate* ridge (1000 feet above the sea), and then descend into the *Deva* valley. You come to

Elgoibar (22 miles from Zaraus, and 38 from San Sebastian), near the saline springs of *Alzola*. Elgoibar contains 2000 inhabitants, has a good inn, and mineral waters.

You now cross a high table-land, with immense oaks and beeches. Pass *Eybar* (4600 inhabitants).

Durango (51 miles from San Sebastian) has 2600 inhabitants, and lies in one of the most beautiful plains of Biscaye. Very old church, and pretty walks. The road improves. Sixteen miles from here to

BILBAO (67 miles from San Sebastian by the Loyola valley).

L

3rd. By Villareal and Vergara.

Go by rail to *Zumarraga* (65 miles from Biarritz), separated by the river Urola, from *Villareal* (1000 inhabitants), whence you drive over a ridge to *Vergara* (eight miles), Hotel de las Diligencias, and de la Posta. (4000 inhabitants.) Vergara is surrounded by mountains. In the San Pedro church, see the fine statue of the Agony of Christ, by Montañes. Here the Carlists capitulated, in August, 1839. Diligences every second day to *Durango* (14 miles); whence to *Bilbao*, 16 miles.

Distance from Zumarraga to Bilbao, by Vergara, 38 miles.

4th. By Rail all the way.

Take the *early morning* train from Biarritz to *Miranda* (132 miles, seven hours). You cross the Cantabrian Pyrenees near *Otzaurte* (78 miles from Biarritz), at a height of almost 2000 feet. Very wild scenery. You also go through *Vitoria* (110 miles from Biarritz), the capital of Alava, with a population of 18,710 inhabitants. Hotel de Pallares. Battle of Vitoria, June, 1813.

Miranda has 3000 inhabitants, and is on the Ebro. Fonda del Norte. Here you leave the

Madrid line, and have to wait an hour before starting for Bilbao (65 miles north).

The journey by rail from Miranda to Bilbao is one of the most wonderful in Europe, the scenery being almost Alpine, and the line ascending in one place (*Inoso* station) to 2163 feet, whence it descends, in about 40 miles, to the level of the sea, by the most eccentric curves. It was engineered by Ch. Vignolles, C.E.

The most remarkable town you pass is *Orduña* (Inn, Aduana), with 3240 inhabitants. Beautiful excursions, trout fishing, and superb fall of the *Nervion*, forming a grand cascade, 700 feet high. (See Murray's Hand-book to Spain.)

Orduña is 42 miles from Miranda, and 23 from Bilbao, which is finally reached (four hours from Miranda) after crossing a beautiful plain.

BILBAO is thus 197 miles from Biarritz: time, 11 hours.

5th. *By Sea.*

Steamers leave Bayonne two or three times a week for Bilbao (83 nautical miles). The passage takes about ten hours, including a stoppage at San Sebastian. Price, 1st class, 21 fr.

BILBAO, capital of Biscaye, contains about 35,000 inhabitants, and stands on the right bank of the Nervion, eight miles from the sea. It is a thriving and commercial town, almost surrounded by Scotch-looking hills, forming the very last headlands visible from Biarritz towards the west. One of the four bridges is beautiful. Promenade del *Arenal,* on the river-side. Bull-fights in summer (August). Cock-fights.

Hotels : de las Navarras : della Antonia : del Boulevart, &c., &c. Good club-house.

Boats and omnibuses every hour to *Portugalete* (seven miles), the port of Bilbao, and a fashionable sea-bathing place. Grand sea-view, near the church. Three miles from Portugalete are the famous iron mines of *Somorrostro.*

PAMPLONA.

1st. *By Rail.*

The distance from the Biarritz station to Pamplona is 116 miles. You first go 83 miles on the Madrid line, as far as *Alsasua,* whence

33 miles to Pamplona. By leaving Biarritz station early in the morning, you reach Pamplona at 3.40 P.M. (See map.) For description as far as Alsasua ("buffet"), see page 138. From here to Pamplona the line crosses a hilly and well-watered country, with high peaks in the distance.

2nd. By Coach, over the Col de Maya.

It is a beautiful drive of 65 miles from Bayonne (67 from Biarritz). Before the opening of the railway by Irun, diligences used to run regularly between Bayonne and Pamplona; but although they still go sometimes, they are no longer to be counted upon. They left from the "Porte d'Espagne" (south end of Bayonne), and performed the journey in one day, stopping for breakfast at Elizondo. Better take a carriage at Biarritz, and either sleep at Elizondo (30 miles), or have a change of horses there.

You cross the Pyrenees east of *La Rhune*, the picturesque and most conspicuous summit rising nearly due south of Biarritz.

(Another carriage-road, but much less frequented, though equally interesting, leaves

Béhobie, the last town in France as you go to Madrid (see Chap. IX.), and goes due south to Pamplona along the right bank of the Bidassoa. It is as long as the other. (See map.)

To go by the Maya col, leave Biarritz by the Cambo road (see Chap. VII.), and follow it until it divides (13 miles), at a mile beyond *Ustaritz.* Here, leaving on the left the well-known Cambo road, you go to the right, and begin a long but gradual, and more than once interrupted, ascent of eight miles, through a very wild country, resembling a desert of ferns, though here and there it is wooded.

After *Espelette* (16 miles from Biarritz, see Chap. VII.), you go up and down for three miles and reach *Ainhoue,* the last village in France. Custom-house. It is a most unnatural frontier, the division of waters being several miles farther south; but this anomaly is common in the Pyrenees, and generally to the advantage of Spain. A bridge on the Nivelle (two miles beyond Ainhoue, and 21 miles from Biarritz), forms the frontier.

(For description of Ainhoue, or Ainhoa, see Chap. XII.) Look N.W. towards the sea.

You now reach *Urdax*, in Spain. Posada de la Toreta. (See Chap. XII.) It was by Urdax that Don Carlos both entered Spain (1834) and left it (1839) a fugitive.

Gently rising on and between barren summits, with a grand view behind, towards the plains of Bayonne, you make your way to the Col de *Maya* (26 miles from Biarritz; under 1600 feet high).

In 1813 the *Col de Maya* was carried by the French, after a bloody engagement; but their defeat at *Sorauren* compelled them to abandon it. "So dreadful was the slaughter at Maya, that it is said the advancing enemy was actually stopped by the heaped mass." (*Napier.*)

Beyond the Col, you go down on the southern slopes of the Pyrenees to the village of *Maya*, and a mile lower down you will see to the west the bare summit of *Achuela*, or *Atchiota*, where King Joseph spent his last night in Spain. You cross several streams, which, soon uniting, form one of the sources of the Bidassoa (Chap. IX.).

"These bleak and exposed heights," says Murray's Guide, "were held, in July, 1813, by

General Stewart, when Soult attempted to relieve Pamplona."

Elizondo (1300 inhabitants, and 30 miles from Biarritz) is the capital of the very fertile valley of *Baztan*, which runs N. and S. for 24 miles, and contains about 8000 inhabitants. There is a tolerable inn at Elizondo (de Estevan Fort) where you can sleep. This village was several times taken and lost by the Carlists.

As you descend the Basque valley of the Baztan, the mountains become less bleak; you find woods of oak, beech, and chestnut, cottages, and clear streams with trout. Before *Almandoz* (40 miles from Biarritz, and 1360 feet in height) you cross a marble bridge, and then travelling due south through dense forests of beech, passing the *Venta de Velate*, once a Templar chapel, you once more begin to ascend in zigzags until you reach the

Port de Velate (3350 feet), beyond which the descent is rapid, for in 11 miles you go down 1750 feet to *Olague*. Road is cut through the rock.

You now leave the Basque country, and the type of the natives is quite altered.

Sorauren (62 miles from Biarritz), although only a very small village, has a great name in history, as it was there that in 1813, Soult was beaten by the Duke of Wellington after a very sanguinary conflict, which cost the French 3000 killed or wounded, and the Allies about as many.

From hence, on foot or riding, you might go (N.E.) to *Roncevaux* (16 miles), whence Soult made a furious, and for a time successful, descent on the British army (1813).

PAMPLONA (Pompeiopolis) is a wonderfully old city, rebuilt by Pompey nearly 2000 years ago! Capital of Navarre, it now contains 23,000 inhabitants. Living is cheap, but the hotels are bad (del Infante, del Florentino, &c.). It is a well-built, but not very strongly fortified town, standing on a height in the middle of a rich plain. The citadel is to the south-west of the town.

The cathedral, built in 1397 (light Gothic), has beautiful cloisters, and an enormous bell in one of its towers. It is outside the city.

Bull-fights in July and August.

There is a grand and most extensive view from the Promenade de la Taconera.

CHAPTER XVI.

A RIDING OR WALKING TOUR OF ABOUT TEN DAYS IN THE FRENCH BASQUE COUNTRY.

HAVING now described in detail the popular places round Biarritz, we shall ask the reader to follow us in a longer, and more or less circular, tour of about 230 miles through the Basque plains and mountains, extending from Biarritz to near the *Vallée d'Aspe*, which runs south and north to *Oloron*, and touches the country already described in my previous work, '*Pau and the Pyrenees.*'

If on foot, a knapsack is enough for this tour. A passport is useful.

FIRST DAY.—*Biarritz* to *Bidache* (26 miles). Go to Bayonne (five miles).

From Bayonne you must take the road to Oloron (60 miles; diligences). You go out of Bayonne by its south-eastern suburb, between the Nive and the Adour, and after passing *St. Pierre d'Irube* (one mile and a half), enter the Basque country. Go east. The country is both rich and hilly, and very populous. At a distance of nine miles from Bayonne you pass the village of *Briscous,* a few miles south of the Adour; but before reaching it, see on the left, in the Ardanabia valley, the celebrated salt works of Briscous. There are five large factories (rock salt, very white). You ascend to Briscous (1620 inhabitants). Continue east, up and down, and over two rivers (the second called the *Joyeuse*); the Pyrenees (S. and S.E.) look very grand.

At 11 miles from Bayonne, you leave on your right (south) the road leading (two miles and a half) to *Labastide-Clairence,* a Basque village, with a colony of Jews.

(*N.B.*—Near this village, on the Ayherre territory, and close to a house called Lucuya, "*lucus,*" are still seen, in a gorge once wooded, the stones of a *Cromlech,* where the Druids used to perform their rites.)

Bardos is 16 miles from Bayonne. Curious church, and château de Gramont, on a hill. Traces of camps in the neighbourhood. You now descend towards the pretty river *Bidouze.*

Bidache is a Basque town on the left bank of it (21 miles from Bayonne, 26 from Biarritz). See the ruins, on a bold hill, of the castle of *Grammont*, burnt in 1793. The Dukes of Grammont are buried in the church. Bidache was taken by assault and sacked by the Spaniards in 1623. Three miles N.W. of Bidache, the smooth and transparent river Bidouze, softly flows under the picturesque ruins of *Guiche*, well seen from the Bayonne and Pau Railway. Some trains stop there (*Came-guiche*; 15 miles from Bayonne).

Bidache reminds one of Henri IV. and the beautiful *Corisande*, Countess of Guiche, whose attachment to him lasted as long as her life; but whom he refused to marry, although the promise to do so was written with his blood. This unhappy and forsaken beauty died in 1620.

Cardinal Mazarin and Napoleon III. were also visitors to Bidache. South of it, one of the countless roads of the Basque country runs to *St. Palais* (15 miles), over wild and almost uninhabited moors. (See map.) (Bidache is only six miles from *Peyrehorade*, a railway station 21 miles from Bayonne.)

SECOND DAY.—Bidache to Salies, and thence to Sauveterre (in all, 21 miles). Going nearly

due east, through *Came*, you reach (eight
miles from Bidache) the village of *Labastide-
Villefranche*, with an awful dungeon; and here,
leaving on the right (south) the road to St.
Palais (11 miles), go north-east, and cross the
gave of Oloron, which falls into the gave of
Pau at Peyrehoradé, about eight miles to the
N.W. Observe ruins of fortifications. A
short mile will then take you to *Caresse*,
whence it is four good miles (east) to

Salies, a town of over 5000 inhabitants,
famous for its salt spring. Several hotels.
Its population is steadily decreasing, by emigration to America. There are traces of
camps, or *casteras* in the neighbourhood.
Excellent hams, called " Bayonne hams."

Salies is only five miles from *Puyôo* and
from *Baigts*, two stations on the Bayonne and
Pau Railway, 30 and 34 miles from the
former.

From Salies to Sauveterre (south) it is
seven miles, over a wide hill.

Sauveterre (1500 inhabitants) lies on the
right bank of the gave of Oloron. Ramparts
in ruins. It was besieged by the Prince of
Orange (see Ad. Joanne's 'Itinéraire des Py-

rénées'). The church is worth seeing. For the fights in this district (1814), see Napier, book xxiv. You are in Béarn, not in the Basque country, which only begins a few miles south-west of Sauveterre, on the St. Palais road.

N.B.—Sauveterre to St. Palais is 9 miles (S.W.). *St. Palais* is a Basque town of 1688 inhabitants (*Donapalena*), in the charming valley of the Bidouze. Hôtel de la Poste. There was a mint there formerly. It is 20 miles from St. Jean Pied de Port, and about the same from the station of Peyrehorade, on the Bayonne and Pau Railway, 21 miles from Bayonne.

Sauveterre to Mauléon, up the Saison Valley, is 14 miles. *Mauléon* is also a Basque town, of nearly 2000 inhabitants. Two hotels (*de la Maréchale* and *Habiague*). It is 27 miles from Orthez (a station on the Bayonne and Pau Railway), 9 from Tardets, 24 from St. Jean Pied de Port. (*Maleo, Malus leo.*) It is on the turbulent stream *Saison*, and is the capital of the Souletains (*Sibilates* of Pliny). See the ruins of its once fortified castle, on a very steep hill (right bank of the stream). There was fierce fighting there during the wars of religion. There is a curious church at Mauléon, with three little spires in a line, perhaps meant to symbolize the Trinity (?) This architectural arrangement is very common in Basque churches.

At Mauléon were held the "General Assemblies," or "States" of Soule.

It was the birth-place of Henri Spondé, a famous Calvinist, born in 1568, who became a Catholic, and finally bishop of Pamiers; also of Oyhenart, Basque historian.

The Pyrenees here become mere hills, and die away on the plains. The drive from Mauléon to Tardets (9 miles south) is beautiful. Observe the beds of ancient lakes, of which the absence is now so conspicuous in the Basque country.

THIRD DAY.—Sauveterre to Oloron, along the gave (23 miles). Always follow up the left bank of the river, which you only cross at Oloron itself. The villages you pass are almost countless, so populous is this interesting and fertile valley.

At 10 miles from Sauveterre, just before crossing *Sus*, you can turn to the left, and cross the gave to *Navarreinx*, a once fortified town, where you had better stop for breakfast (25 miles from Pau, by *Monein*, and a very pretty drive). From here to Oloron (in fact, from Sauveterre also) there is a road on either bank. If you choose the left bank, you leave on your right, a few miles before Oloron, the village of *Montmour*, with an old tower attributed to the Sarrasins; and you at last reach Oloron by its western suburb of Ste. Marie.

During the whole of this journey, which, from Biarritz, a good pedestrian can easily perform in three moderate days' walking, you never cease to see the Pyrenees on your right, on a line parallel to your own, and gradually increasing in height from west to east. Very often glimpses may be had of the graceful monarch of these regions, the Pic *d'Anie* (8216 feet), the loftiest in the Western Pyrenees, and of very easy ascent. It rises south of *Navarreinx* (30 miles. See *Pau and the Pyrenees*). West of this peak the Pyrenees begin to sink, but very gradually; and nothing in its way can be more beautiful, especially on a summer evening, than this jagged line of blue or snowy mountains, often black with forests, standing like a wall between Spanish Navarre and the Basque plains, and dipping towards the west, with the sun, into the Atlantic.

You can drive the whole of the journey just described.

Oloron (*Iluron*), though beyond the limits of the Basque country (see map), is often supposed to mean in Basque "Town of good waters." It is a gay little town, of 9000 inhabitants, 20 miles south-west of Pau, and has a good hotel (Condesse). Diligences to Pau daily. Two noisy and clear Pyrenæan torrents, or *gaves*, meet here, under the grassy hill where the town proudly stands, only a few miles from the line of lofty peaks whose rocks and woods seem to steam in the sun, and already rise to thousands of feet above the plains.

Oloron was long a Bishopric. It is now a thriving town, although it was plundered and half ruined, in 1694, by the Spaniards. Great markets. It is two miles long, being very narrow. See the *Ste. Croix* church, built in 1080.

Diligences to Orthez, St. Palais, St. Christau, Bédous, Pau, &c., &c.

FOURTH DAY.—Oloron to Tardets. (Diligences as far as *Aramits*, nine miles.)

Leaving Oloron in a south-westerly direction, on a capital carriage-road, you first proceed through a very fertile but flat country, with the blue Pyrenees standing up on your left, like a bold and rugged wall, almost covered with boundless forests abounding in game. Along the road there are poplars, small oaks, heath, meadows, and villas; and a little beyond, the plain begins to undulate as you approach the Pyrenees, bleak little hills rising here and there like waves.

Six miles take you to a bridge, where you cross the *Vert*, a clear and modest stream descending from the south, down the *Barétous* valley, famous for its cows, its scenery, and the many traces the Sarrasins have left in it. The view from this bridge, looking south, is quite Swiss-like.

After *Féas* (six miles and a half) you soon reach *Aramits* (nine miles from Oloron).

Now you leave the plains, and enter a very hilly country, facing abrupt and rocky peaks to the south, where the *Anie* (8216 feet), and its almost always snowy summit, stands out most boldly.

South of *Lannes* (11 miles from Oloron), there are, in the autumn, huge nets, or *palombières*, for catching wild doves, as they fly over the Pyrenees.

Then you gently rise to the Col de *Lapixe*, and go down a long and steepish hill to the village of *Montory*, beyond which you enter the Basque country, with its mountains rising here to about 4000 feet. Ferns everywhere, green slopes, and white farms scattered all over them.

Montory has iron mines, and looks wealthy

(15 miles from Oloron). Beyond this you go west, on a more level road, to *Tardets* (19 miles from Oloron).

As you enter Tardets, the " Hotel des Voyageurs" is on your left. The scenery is singular, but picturesque ; all the lines are as broken and tortuous as in a volcanic country. To the west, conical and almost countless little hills rise in confusion, and far beyond, the Pic des *Escaliers* (4900 feet, W.S.W.) rears its brown and barren slopes, whilst to the south, 12 or 13 miles distant, the peaks of *Ste. Engrace* reach 6000 feet, and even more.

Immediately round Tardets the land is fertile, being watered by the foaming waves of the *Saison,* but the circle of hills beyond is rather bare.

The climate is strange and changeable : hot south winds are frequent in autumn, and bring rain ; but the north wind often blows above it, and the clouds are seen to struggle between them.

Tardets (1000 inhabitants) has imposing and handsome houses, and a pretty new church. Here was born Ohaho, the elegant Basque historian.

Living is very cheap: five shillings a day suffices for luxury.

N.N.E. of Tardets there rises a hill called *La Madeleine* (2700 feet), and well worth an ascent. A poor chapel stands on the top, and it contains a marble slab, with a Roman inscription. There are yearly pilgrimages.

To ascend *La Madeleine* (four miles to the top), you first rise N.E. on a cart-road for about 45 minutes, then continue N.W. on a barren and windy moor for half an hour. The view from the summit is grand indeed, although you cannot see the sea. The plains are boundless, and you can see very clearly, not only the *Pic du Midi de Pau*, but also that of *Bigorre*, fully 60 miles away. Even the humble hills of *Lourdes* are quite plain (50 miles due east). But the *Anie* (8216 feet), being so near (S.E.), is the real monarch of this grand chain. The Pic d'*Orrhy* (6660 feet), its rival, also towers very nobly in the S.W.

You can descend westward, more abruptly, and thus save a mile. Here are magnificent chestnuts. But the ascent of *La Madeleine* is deceptive as to distance. It is much farther than it looks.

Altogether, Tardets would make excellent head-quarters for good pedestrians. It is nine miles from *Mauléon*, a town north of it : diligences daily. Two short miles north of Tardets, in the lovely valley of the Saison, on the left of the road, stands the château of Count de Montréal. Built in 1662–4 by M. de Trevilles (one of the heroes of Dumas's *Trois Mousquetaires*), and once visited by the Duchess de Berry, it is called *Trois-Villes*, and is a charming place, surrounded with trees and fields, where the *Saison* winds and roars between a double row of wild hills, whose bleak points appear above the trees. In fact, on all sides, mountains, great or low, frown upon the lawns of Trois-Villes, its trees, and its rustic bridges. In the south, the view is almost Alpine.

N.B.—From Tardets to *Roncal*, a Spanish village due south of it, on the other side of the Pyrenees, it is nine hours' walk or ride over the *Col de la Pix* (4600 feet), exactly due south of Tardets: this is midway. Pretty church at Roncal (500 inhabitants), where, in the eighth and ninth centuries, the Moors suffered bloody defeats.

FIFTH DAY.—Tardets to Larrau and the Pic d'Orrhy.

It is 11 miles from Tardets to Larrau (S.W.), the last village in France on that side, and you can drive it; the last mile only being difficult for carriages.

First go south on the right bank of the Saison. The scenery is rather tame and uninteresting, but at *Licq* (four miles) 'it improves. Here the torrent forms a small cataract. A mile beyond Licq the valley divides, the left branch running up to *Ste. Engrace*, a village of 1200 inhabitants, most romantically perched high up in the Uhaïtxa valley. You must ride or walk to it (two and a half hours), and the only dwelling you pass is the custom-house. The natives are all Basques, though very fair, says M. Ad. Joanne. According to the Rev. Haristoy, already quoted (Chap. IV.), " the Ste. Engrace monastery and abbey were already flourishing in the eleventh century. The monks fulfilled, among other duties, that of guiding travellers through those wild and inhospitable regions. The Basque country had many of these institutions, half hotels, half monasteries. Tardets (in Basque, *Atharatce*, 'a refuge for strangers') owed its origin to one of them. Of the monastery of Ste. Engrace nothing now remains but a handsome church of the purest Romano-Byzantine style."

(*N.B.*—It is only five hours' walk from Ste. Engrace to the top of the Pic d'*Anie* (S.E., 8216 feet), which you ascend by its western side. View splendid.)

Continuing your journey to Larrau, and leaving on your left the Ste. Engrace mule-track, you come to the junction of both tor-rents (Uhaïtxa and Saison); this "meeting of the waters" is five miles from Tardets. Cross-ing the Saison on a handsome bridge, and looking up (S.E.) towards the *Arlas* summits (6700 feet), you now enter a narrow, tortuous, and densely-wooded gorge, and gradually get imprisoned in a perfect maze of middle-sized mountains, with cheerful houses perched at every height on their slopes or summits. In fact, the gorge becomes so contracted, that you can easily throw a stone across it; there is just room for the road and torrent, which is half bridged over by the straight branches of mighty chestnuts and oaks, under whose leaves the furious stream boils, and whitens every rock. Occasionally, but only for a few moments, you get glimpses of high peaks to the south (*Bimbalette*, 6000 feet).

At a mile before Larrau there is a steep

ascent, detestable for carriages, and turning towards every point of the compass. After passing a wretched inn, you go westward, observing on the right (north), on the other side of the torrent, a broken and jagged precipice rising to nearly 1000 feet.

At last you reach the plateau of *Larrau* (11 miles from Tardets, and about 2500 feet above the sea-level?). In the west, modest hills undulate, emerging from a sea of forests (*Iraty*).

Larrau is a neat and compact village of 1200 souls. The inn (*Topino*) is not at all bad. Iron-foundry two miles to the west. Waterfall of *Holsat*, two hours to the east, in the forest of the same name.

The *Pic d' Orrhy* (6660 feet), well seen from the Bayonne country, can easily be reached in three hours (on foot) from Larrau, but is not seen from it. It rises to the S.W. of it. It is a noble peak, though so humble, and chamois are found on its rocks. Slopes of grass will take you to the top by its south-eastern side. You first ascend from Larrau to the *Col de Larrau* (4500 feet, S.W.), passing before the *St. Joseph* chapel. Riding or walking, two hours will bring you to the *Col*, whence to the top of the Orrhy it takes a good hour. The Atlantic is quite visible from the summit.

N.B.—A very easy descent of two hours, in a south-westerly direction, would take you from the Col de Larrau to the Spanish village of *Ochagavia* (1800 inhabitants), at the foot of the *Musguilde* mountain, where stands an *hermitage*. Wretched inns; but lovely view south, down the Salazar Valley. Ruins of two castles. (See Ad. Joanne's admirable 'Itinéraire des Pyrénées.')

SIXTH DAY.—Tardets to Ahusky. It is about 12 miles. Direction, west. You can drive for four miles, and ride the rest of the way. Start W.S.W. from Tardets, crossing the Saison on a pretty bridge, and facing the *Pic des Escaliers* (4900 feet). After passing several villages, better leave the carriage-road (three miles) on your left, and begin to ascend on the right, on barren, stony slopes, rather bad for a horse. You thus follow the left bank (right side as you go up) of a gloomy gorge. Houses and culture gradually disappear; it is like a moor of Donegal. Nothing is heard, and there is no water; ferns extend everywhere. Two hours and a half (walking) from Tardets will place you on a *col* with beech-trees; and there you meet a track coming up, on the right, from Mauléon (same distance as Tardets). In the forests stretching below on that side gipsies are found.

Go to the west, in a level and pretty straight ravine, without a torrent, between a double row of fern-covered hills. See a *cabane*, then another, on your right. It is a strange and dreary place, 3000 feet above the sea-level. There is not a sound, and no view; you go from east to west through a kind of dismal gallery, all brown with ferns. At last, at the western end of it, opens a *col*, or depression, to the right of which are seen five or six small houses, one of them rose-coloured, which is the inn of Ahusky. What a relief, what a blessing in bad weather! for there is not a tree or a rock near, beneath which you could get shelter. Height, 3000 feet. It is nearly four hours' walking from Tardets to Ahusky, most unquestionably one of the strangest places in all the Pyrenees. The wilderness is appalling. But you can get a bed and a dinner in the inn, even in mid-winter, although the snow is sometimes five feet deep! North of the inn there is a little hill, almost 4000 feet above the sea-level; on a clear winter day the Atlantic is visible from this point (40 miles away, N.W.). From the inn itself the view is very grand also towards the south and east; the *Pic des Escaliers* especially (4900 feet) looks very bold and majestic (S.S.W.), rising in solemn solitude, behind long and waving slopes, all covered with ferns. Wolves and bears are common in these windy deserts, as the shepherds know but too well.

Left of the *Escaliers* there is an easy passage to Larrau (three hours); there is much going up and down, but no climbing to speak of.

Under your feet, to the south-east, runs a valley with dense woods, rushing streams and verdure; and due south of Ahusky, only seven miles distant, the *Pic d'Orrhy* proudly stands, humiliating all its neighbours. To the S.S.E. there is a long line of peaks (*Arlas*, *Anie*, &c.), generally covered with snow.

Far away to the east you can just see the *Bigorre* mountains (80 miles).

On the whole, a few days may be pleasantly spent at Ahusky in a bracing and splendid climate. There is a famous spring within a hundred yards of it; you can drink with impunity whole bottles of this most peculiar water, fifty glasses a day being a common dose! It is good for fever, digestion, and the nervous system. It is said to bubble in the glass like soda-water (?).

A good pedestrian could walk in about eight hours from Ahusky to the Spanish village of *Ochagavia* (alluded to above), by penetrating through the magnificent forests of Iraty, probably the largest in all the Pyrenees. The direction is south-west, as far as the frontier, where you enter Spain by the *Port d'Aborreta* (4000 feet), west of the Pic d'Orrhy. Then you steer due south, and go down in three hours to Ochagavia. But no one, not even a member of the Alpine Club, ought to attempt this excursion without a compass and a map. Once lost in the forest of Iraty nothing but a compass could possibly save you.

Geologists ought to visit, near Ahusky, the deep natural holes or wells, beneath whose gloomy depths torrents are heard roaring.

N.B.—Biarritz tourists should certainly not fail to go to Ahusky, a curious place indeed, with much game, no summer heat, and all the necessaries of life. It is a little over 50 miles south-east of Biarritz, passing by Cambo and St. Jean Pied de Port; you might sleep in both places comfortably.

SEVENTH DAY.—Ahusky to St. Jean Pied de Port. This is a journey of 18 miles; and you can ride the whole distance.

From Ahusky go west, on a mule-track, ascending a little. You soon find yourself on a brown and gloomy wilderness of heather, with a few rocks only to break its distressing monotony. It is indeed a melancholy place in bad weather. There are deep holes right and left, with water running in. Towards the north-east you catch a few glimpses of great blue plains in the distance, the only thing which can remind you of your height (3000 feet). Look back (S.E.) at the majestic peak d'*Anie* (8216 feet). Wolves are common here in autumn and winter.

Westward you now see three bare little summits, rising a few hundred feet above your own level. Steer to the left of the middle one, the highest, *Aphanicé* (4200 feet). An hour from Ahusky will make you reach three good *cabanes*: plenty of rocks; no trees. Grand view below, west and north-west. You begin to descend in earnest, first west, then north-west: bad road for mules. Once on the western side of the rocky arête of the Aphanicé, you get a most extensive view towards the north-west, where a valley, studded with villages, and green as emerald, runs far away fully 2000 feet under your own level. Its trees, torrents, and fields form a lovely contrast with the solemn and bare summits around you. But St. Jean Pied de Port is not yet in sight. The soil here is very ferruginous, and quite red. Do not go down straight into the gorge below you; it is longer. Keep to the left, on an undulating, weather-beaten, and round ridge, where you descend very gradually, by a succession of terraces going due west.

Passing under a few chestnuts, you come at last (2.30 from Ahusky) to the *Mendive* commune, where, on level ground, you meet a carriage-road.

(*N.B.*—From hence you might reach on foot, in eight short hours, the Spanish village of *Ochagavia*, already mentioned, by always going *south*, crossing the enormous forest of *Iraty*, then the torrent of the same name, and finally the almost unexplored, but humble, *Abody* mountains, south of which a short descent of about two hours would take you to Ochagavia.)

After *Mendive*, continuing north-west towards St. Jean Pied de Port, you pass near

some unimportant iron-works, and reach the
village of *Lecumberry* ("new house"). Decent
inn on the left, opposite the custom-house.
(Three hours from Ahusky.) Four miles more,
on an excellent road, and through a beautiful
country, like the hilly parts of Ireland, take
you to *St. Jean le Vieux*, where leaving on
your right the fine road to *St. Palais* (18
miles), you turn abruptly to the left (west).
From here, two miles and a half will land you
at St. Jean Pied de Port. (Observe on a commanding hill to your left the neat and imposing château d'*Irumberry*.)

St. Jean Pied de Port is a fortified little town
of about 2000 inhabitants, almost surrounded
with barren hills, and in the very heart of the
French Basque country. It is only five miles
from Spain. *Hotel de France.* The citadel is
a strong one; the streets are very narrow, but
clean. Three streams (or *Nives*) meet here.
It only belongs to France since 1659, and was
fortified by Vauban. See the church, and do
not fail to taste the chocolate.

St. Jean Pied de Port is 40 miles from
Bayonne, by *Irissary*, *Helette*, and *Attisane* (diligences daily); but only 35 by *Louhossoa* and

Cambo (carriage-road), and 42 by *St. Etienne de Baïgorry, Bidarray*, and *Cambo*.

The diligences, which are wretched, leave Bayonne from the Hôtel des Basques, near St. André.

N.B.—From St. Jean Pied de Port to Mauléon it is 24 miles by the high road. Take the *St. Palais* road (N.E.). At five miles you cross *Lacarre*, where Marshal Harispe is buried. He distinguished himself at Jena, Friedland, Saragossa, and in 1814. At seven miles, after passing a little *col*, you go down (N.E.) through a dreary valley, to *Larceveau* (10 miles). Ruins of walls, destroyed during the wars of religion, says M. A. Joanne. Here leave the St. Palais road, and turn sharply to the south-east, ascending the *Bidouze* valley. Trees re-appear. The beautiful little river Bidouze springs from a grotto, five miles higher up. You soon leave it, after passing *St. Just* (18 miles), and rise to the left. You then reach a windy plateau, covered with ferns, and with a splendid view; the Pyrenees rise south to 6000 feet, and the sea, though 40 miles distant, is seen in the north-west. Now descend through a charming valley, by *Musculdy* (20 miles), to *Mauléon* (24 miles), for description of which, see above.

EIGHTH DAY.—St. Jean Pied de Port to Roncevaux is 17 miles (eight by carriage).

This is part of the projected road from Pau to Pampeluna. Passing by the church at St. Jean Pied de Port, and there turning to the right, you rise gently on an excellent road, along the right bank of an insignificant but clear little river, or " nive," called *Arnéguy*. (See high up on the hills to the left, the old and shorter track to Roncevaux, by the *Bentarte* col.)

The banks of the torrent of Arnéguy are green, wooded, and populous: but the hills above them are uninteresting and barren.

At four miles, you pass the village of *Benta*, with very white houses. Here you are still in France, but the left bank of the torrent becomes Spanish. The Arnéguy, imprisoned between slopes of intense green, becomes more noisy, and large chestnuts soon make their appearance above.

At the village of *Arnéguy* (five miles from St. Jean Pied de Port : about fifty houses) you cross the stream on a wooden bridge, and enter Spain. Almost the whole population is composed of smugglers. The road now ascends in long zigzags to

Valcarlos or *Luzaïde* (eight miles from St. Jean Pied de Port), a long village with a few very handsome houses. The carriage-road, for the present, stops here : and you must walk or get a mule to go to Roncevaux.

N

In the Bathing Establishment (*d'Hydro-therapia*) you can live comfortably. There is also an inn beyond the church (left of the road). See the *Plaza " de la Constitucion,"* a pompous name indeed, considering it is only built on one side!

The scenery is tame, but pastoral; there are hills, verdure, and shade almost everywhere. The climate is excellent, not too hot in summer. You are in Spain, but the opposite bank is still in France. It is only at two miles beyond Valcarlos that both banks are Spanish.

The mule-track you now follow is in a lamentable condition, but the scenery improves, and you enter forests of colossal chestnuts, worth measuring: there are none like them in all the Pyrenees. After a few miles, the valley stops against a *cirque,* or immense wall of hills, all black with dense forests, where a solitary house, white as a fresh flake of snow, alone glitters amidst the gloom. The road passes just under it, as it ascends the wooded cirque. But before beginning this ascent, your track divides. Go to the left, and here cross the torrent. (The track to the right leads in two hours to *Burguete.*)

As you ascend south in long, endless zigzags, under chestnuts and beech, on an atrocious
road, the northern horizon becomes more imposing towards the lovely regions of Cambo
and the Nive. But round you it is dark as
night, under those massive trees where nothing
moves or shines. After passing the white
house mentioned above, which stands just midway up the hill, you must turn sharply to the
left. At last you reach the

Col de Roncevaux (3700 feet, 16 miles from
St. Jean Pied de Port), leaving on your right
the crests of the *Lindux* (see below). There is a
deserted chapel or *hermitage* on the top of the
col, south of which the view is very strange.
The whole country, as far as you can see,
scarcely sinking below a level of 3000 feet,
looks like a vast table-land, with wooded hills
running everywhere on its surface like the
Atlantic billows. The whole horizon seems
one mass of forests, without a house in sight.
But here and there a few acres of beautiful
verdure shine in those enormous woods, and
streams murmur, though you cannot see them.

The group of barren peaks east of the Col
de Roncevaux is vaguely called *Altabiscar.*

N 2

Here the rear-guard of Charlemagne's army, retreating from Spain, was exterminated by the Basques in 778, and the brave paladin *Roland* (or Rotlandus) lost his life. In 1813 Soult crossed the col with a powerful force, and succeeded in rolling back the British troops towards the Spanish village of *Sorauren;* but here his advantage ended in a sanguinary defeat.

It was also through Roncevaux (says Murray) that the Black Prince led his legions in 1367, to the victory of Navarrete.

Chestnuts here disappear, or nearly so, and are replaced by beech-trees. You descend one mile, and suddenly find yourself at

Roncevaux (Rossida vallis in Latin, *Roncesvalles* in Spanish), a group of houses standing 3000 feet above the sea-level. Passing through the convent buildings, whose frowning and gloomy walls remind you of a fortress, you reach the inn, almost the last house on the left-hand side. Clean beds and good living, for a few francs a day.

Visit the church (Gothic) and the convent of Augustine monks, the cloisters, &c. The supposed boots, gauntlets, &c., of the great paladin, of Ariosto's hero, *Roland,* are shown in the sacristy.

This strange and imposing plateau is one of the least known regions in all the Pyrenees, although you could live there comfortably for months, avoiding the summer heats, away from all the luxury, necessities, tumult, and foolishness of crowded towns and watering-places. What a fine retreat for a philosopher !!

It is two short miles from Roncevaux to the village of *Burguete,* whence two roads lead to Pamplona ; one for diligences (which start every morning), and about 30 miles long ; another, much shorter, and more to the west, but only practicable for horses or mules (about 25 miles).

In round numbers, it is 50 miles from St. Jean Pied de Port to Pamplona (whence to Biarritz by railway, about nine hours. See Chap. XV.).

NINTH DAY.—Roncevaux to Aldudes and St. Etienne de Baïgorry (in all, 21 miles).

From Roncevaux, if you look to the west, you will observe a sharp little summit, over-topping the vast forests which girdle it ; to the right of it lies the track to the Aldudes, a French Basque village. Take a boy for a guide as far as the *col* (one franc). Leaving Roncevaux in a westerly direction, by an avenue of ash-trees, see *Burguete* in the distance (south), glittering in the sun, surrounded by a sea of trees. A compass and a map are extremely useful in these unfrequented regions. There is a tortuous mule-track which rises gently at first through the forest; you steer N.W., then W., after crossing a sluggish stream. It is a short and easy hour from Roncevaux to the *Col de Macharica* (3400 feet), a sort of wide ridge, covered with grass, and running south-west of the *Pic de Lindux* (4100 feet), on the summit of which a severe engagement took place in 1813, between Ross's column and Marshal Reille. "Brave men," says Napier, "fell on both sides; but numbers prevailing, these daring soldiers were pushed back again by the French."

From the summit of this much-exposed ridge, the view is striking towards France, where the peak of *La Rhune* (Chap. XIII.) appears to advantage in the north-west. Here again, as in so many parts of the Pyrenees, you are still in Spain, although north of the crest-dividing waters. Observe a green and grassy col far below you (N.W.); there you must go down through the forest, making a long semicircle to the right. You soon re-enter France, pass the custom-house, and go through a very open and rather bleak country, all torn with gorges and ravines, whence issue the sources of the Nive, which joins the Adour at Bayonne, after a course (almost due north) of about 50 miles. You stand hundreds of feet above the *right* bank of one of those torrents, which all unite their waters 2000 feet lower down. Once on the little col spoken of just now (45 minutes from the main ridge you passed), you cross a narrow spur, and suddenly find yourself on the *left* side of another gorge, and at a still greater height above the torrent. Here comes a steep descent, over hideous and large ravines, full of loose stones. Once on a level with the torrent, you pass a big house, re-ascend a little to the left, where you once more find culture—chestnuts and fields—and cross a second spur. The road improves, and you reach at last the right side of a third gorge, leading down in gentle slopes

to the valley and village of Aldudes. There
is a lovely view below (N.W.), where a line
of white Basque houses stand sparkling in the
sun, between meadows and poplar-trees, lining
the cradle of the Nive. Everything breathes
cleanliness, comfort, and happiness, not to say
wealth.

See (north) a tall and brown mountain
(4500 feet), the *Pic de Hausas*. The others
are ugly, rounded, and vulgar.

Once upon level ground, the first village you
reach is *Urepel* (three hours' walk or ride
from Roncevaux): and here there is once
more a carriage-road on the right bank of the
Nive. (You must therefore ride or walk all
the journey just described, from Valcarlos,
through Roncevaux, to Urepel.)

Two miles and a half beyond Urepel, you
enter the *Aldudes* (11 miles from Roncevaux).
There is a good hotel south of the church,
close to the bridge. 1226 inhabitants. A
small "*cabriolet*," holding two passengers,
carries the mails daily to *Irissary*, on the
Bayonne and St. Jean Pied de Port road. The
French and Spanish Basques often meet at
Aldudes, to fight out the *jeu de paume*.

It is a long, straggling village, and, like most Basque villages, apparently endless. There is an easy mule-track, leading in three hours from the Aldudes to the Spanish village of *Elizondo* (N.W.; see Chap. XV.), over the Col de *Berdaritz* (2300 feet), carried by the French in 1794.

It is 46 miles from Aldudes to Biarritz, by Bidarray and Cambo, but only 40 by Elizondo and the Col de Maya (see Chap. XV.). To drive the whole distance you must take the former road, which is far more interesting.

On the hills south-east of Aldudes there are "*Pantières*" to catch ringdoves.

As you go on, you now fall into an excellent carriage-road, descending N.N.E. the valley of the Nive, alternately on either bank. The gorge is so narrow that it often becomes a mere ravine with a torrent, and it is easy to throw a stone across. Chestnuts, ferns, and rocks more or less adorn the conical and pretty little peaks rising on every side. The road is often red in colour, and winds like a snake. Five miles beyond Aldudes you pass a *foundry*, and some copper and silver mines, with upwards of fifty galleries or wells, often

attributed to the Romans. See (east) the peak
of *Adarca* (4300 feet). Cultivation improves
as you approach

St. Etienne de Baïgorry, 10 miles from
Aldudes, 21 from Roncevaux, 7 from St. Jean
Pied de Port, 36 from Biarritz, by Cambo.
2500 inhabitants. Inn, *Bergugnan*, at the
north end of the town, near the "jeu de
paume."

During the last century, cannon used to be
cast at or near St. Etienne. Antimony and
iron are found in the neighbourhood.

The town is in a valley, as smiling and
green as possible, but all the hills near it are
bare and grey. It is the birth-place of
Marshal Harispe.

A mule-track goes over the frontier, west
of St. Etienne de Baïgorry, leading in three
hours to the Spanish village of *Maya* (see
Chap. XV.), whence to Biarritz it is 27 miles
by carriage-road.

TENTH DAY.—St. Etienne de Baïgorry to
Cambo and Biarritz (in all, 36 miles).

From Baïgorry you go down the left bank
of the Nive; nothing very interesting; chest-

nuts, ferns, and modest hills. Seven miles
place you at the junction of the Arnéguy and
the Nive; venerable old bridge covered with
ivy. A little farther on, the gorge opens
upon the fertile plain of *Ossès* (2000 inhabitants). Here where the Nive, transparent as
crystal, flows under a beautiful bridge, you
leave the main road which goes N.E. to *St.
Palais* (20 miles), and follow on the left the
by-road crossing Ossès, on the left bank of
the Nive. It is a carriage-road. At a mile
beyond Ossès, you take the right bank.
Pedestrians can follow the left bank all the
way to Cambo, passing by the *Pas de Roland*
(see Chap. VII.): it looks shorter, but it is
scarcely so, on account of the continual
ups and downs.

The river Nive, your companion, guide, and
friend, is no doubt one of the most attractive
of Pyrenæan torrents, and perhaps the purest
and the most winding; you never know
where it is leading you. When its waters are
calm they are as translucid as glass, and as
green as the leaves floating on their surface,
for there can be no mud or deposits in that
clear bed of rocks. But the Nive runs rapidly

and madly sometimes, when choked between two hills, and shoots right and left like the wind or an arrow, throwing masses of foam upon its green or stony banks.

As you descend towards Bidarray, observe bold peaks to the west, as bare as the sandy summits of the Red Sea. Spain is behind them. But your road is lined with chestnuts, poplars, Indian-corn, box-wood, and oaks. Ten good miles from St. Etienne de Baïgorry take you to

Bidarray, the only filthy place I ever found on Basque soil. Avoid sleeping there. Fine old bridge. "Holy grotto" in the neighbourhood.

Bidarray to Biarritz is 26 miles by Louhossoa, and carriage-road; not much less by the banks of the Nive and the *Pas de Roland.* (Chap. VII.)

Below Bidarray the carriage-road continues down the right bank of the Nive for two miles, then it turns quite away from it to the right, passes over a little *col*, and beyond it, enters the Basque village of *Louhossoa* (manufacture of *Kaolin*, "porcelain clay"), five miles from Cambo.

At Louhossoa (two inns) you join one of the two capital roads from St. Jean Pied de Port to Bayonne; you turn to the left, go down a long hill, recross the Nive on a suspension bridge, and at last reach the village of *Itsatsou* (described in Chap. VII.), north of the Pas de Roland, whence, steering north, you will enter *Cambo* by its western side. Cambo is 21 miles from St. Etienne de Baïgorry, and 11 from Bidarray.

For the road from Cambo to Biarritz (15 miles), see Chap. VII.

So here we are once more in beautiful Biarritz; and we re-enter it without that sadness which often falls upon the soul like a chain or a cloud, when we say good-bye to Nature and Freedom, two things so dear to travellers, and so hard to part with!

INDEX.

INDEX.

LONDON: PRINTED BY EDWARD STANFORD, 6 & 7, CHARING CROSS, S.W.

June, 1873.

LIST OF BOOKS

PUBLISHED BY

EDWARD STANFORD,

6 and 7, CHARING CROSS, LONDON, S.W.,

AGENT, BY APPOINTMENT, FOR THE SALE OF THE ORDNANCE MAPS,
GEOLOGICAL SURVEY MAPS, ADMIRALTY CHARTS, ETC.

ADDERLEY (Sir C. B.).—COLONIAL POLICY and HIS-
TORY—REVIEW of "The COLONIAL POLICY of LORD
J. RUSSELL'S ADMINISTRATION, BY EARL GREY, 1853,"
and of SUBSEQUENT COLONIAL HISTORY. By the Right
Hon. Sir C. B. Adderley, K.C.M.G., M.P. Demy 8vo, cloth, 9s.

AMERICA, NORTH.—NOTES on the GEOGRAPHY of
NORTH AMERICA, PHYSICAL and POLITICAL. Intended
to serve as a Text Book for the Use of Elementary Classes, and as
a Handbook to the Wall Map prepared under the direction of the
Society for Promoting Christian Knowledge, and the
National Society for Promoting the Education of the
Poor. With Coloured Physical Map. Crown 8vo, cloth, 1s.

—— **SOUTH.—NOTES on the GEOGRAPHY of SOUTH**
AMERICA, PHYSICAL and POLITICAL. Intended to serve as
a Text Book for the Use of Elementary Classes, and as a Handbook
to the Wall Map prepared under the direction of the Society for
Promoting Christian Knowledge, and the National
Society for Promoting the Education of the Poor. With
Coloured Physical Map. Crown 8vo, cloth, 1s.

ANDLAU'S (Baron) GRAMMAR and KEY to the GERMAN
LANGUAGE: Being an easy and complete System for acquiring
this useful tongue, with Progressive Exercises, &c. By the Baron
Von Andlau, Director of the German, French, and Classical College,
Clapham Rise, London. Fourth Edition, revised and greatly enlarged.
Demy 12mo, cloth, 3s. 6d.

—— **GERMAN READING BOOK:** Containing Sentences, De-
scriptions, Tales, and Poetry, with the necessary explanations in
English, for the Use of Schools, Private, and Self Instruction. First
Course. Demy 12mo, cloth, 3s. 6d.

—— **GERMAN READING BOOK.** Second Course. Demy
12mo, cloth, 4s. 6d.

BROWNE (W. A., LL.D.).—ARMY TESTS in ARITHMETIC: Being the Questions set to Candidates for Woolwich Direct Commissions, Sandhurst, Commissariat, and Staff College. WITH ANSWERS. Demy 12mo, cloth, 3s. 6d.

—— **CIVIL SERVICE TESTS in ARITHMETIC:** Being Specimens of the more difficult Questions in the Civil Service Reports, with full Solutions. To which are appended the Questions in the Eleventh Report, WITH ANSWERS. Demy 12mo, cloth, 2s. 6d.

—— **ARITHMETICAL QUESTIONS in the 8th CIVIL SERVICE REPORT,** with Solutions. Demy 12mo, 1s.

—— **CIVIL SERVICE GUIDE to HISTORY:** Being the Historical Questions in the Civil Service Reports. Arranged under the several Periods and Reigns to which they belong. Demy 12mo, cloth, 2s. 6d.

—— **CIVIL SERVICE GUIDE to GEOGRAPHY:** Being the Geographical Questions in the Civil Service Reports, showing those that refer to the different Countries. Demy 12mo, 8d.

—— **SPECIMENS of HANDWRITING:** Approved by the Civil Service Commissioners. Demy 8vo, 2d.

CHAMBERS.—HANDBOOK for EASTBOURNE and SEAFORD, and the NEIGHBOURHOOD. By G. F. CHAMBERS, F.R.A.S., of the Inner Temple, Barrister-at-Law; Author of 'Descriptive Astronomy,' &c. Fourth Edition, crown 8vo, 1s.; with Map, 1s. 4d.

CHAPMAN (James, F.R.G.S.).—TRAVELS in the INTERIOR of SOUTH AFRICA, comprising Fifteen Years' Hunting and Trading Experiences; with Journeys across the Continent from Natal to Walvisch Bay, and Visits to Lake Ngami and Victoria Falls. With Maps and numerous Engravings. 2 vols. demy 8vo, cloth, 32s.

CHERPILLOUD'S (Prof. J.) BOOK of VERSIONS; or, Guide to French Translation and Construction. New Edition, revised, by Prof. C. J. DELILLE, late of the City of London School. Demy 12mo, bound, 3s. 6d.

—— **KEY to the ABOVE.—PARTIE FRANÇAISE du LIVRE de VERSIONS;** ou, Guide à la Traduction de l'Anglais en Français. By Prof. C. J. DELILLE. Demy 12mo, bound, 3s. 6d.

EDWARD STANFORD, 6 & 7, CHARING CROSS, S.W.,

CHRONOLOGICAL PICTURES of ENGLISH HISTORY, from the ANCIENT BRITONS to the Reign of QUEEN VICTORIA. A Series of 40 Plates, containing 360 Illustrations, beautifully Tinted, Designed, and Drawn on Stone, by Sir JOHN GILBERT, President of the Society of Painters in Water Colours. With an additional Plate to illustrate the Reign of Queen Victoria, thus continuing the Series up to the Present Time. Each Plate illustrates a period or a reign, and Facsimiles of the Autographs of the Sovereigns and the most distinguished Characters are attached. New Edition. Imperial folio, half-bound morocco, 3*l.*; the Set of Plates in Sheets, 2*l.*; in best Oak Frame, with Glass, 3*l.*; in cheaper Frame, with Glass, 2*l.* 12*s.* 6*d.*; Single Plates, 1*s.* each.

COOK (T. B.).—BRITANNIA ALMANACK, for the Past and Future, comprising a period of 200 years. Price 6*d.*

CRACROFT'S INVESTMENT TRACTS.—AMERICAN RAILWAYS AS INVESTMENTS. By ROBERT GIFFEN. Dedicated to the Members of the London Stock Exchange. Second Edition. Royal 8vo, cloth, 5*s.*

CUMMING.—GUIDE to the ISLE of MAN, its Approaches and Places of Resort, with numerous Walks, Drives, and Excursions; its History, Geology, Botany, &c., &c. By the Rev. J. G. CUMMING, M.A., F.G.S., Vice-Principal of King William's College, Castletown. With Map. Fcap. 8vo, cloth, 4*s.* 6*d.*

DALLY.—GUIDE to JERSEY and GUERNSEY; with Notes on their History, Geology, Climate, Agriculture, Laws, &c. By F. F. DALLY, Esq., Author of an 'Essay on the Agriculture of the Channel Islands.' Third Edition. With Maps. Fcap. 8vo, cloth, 3*s.* 6*d.*; or separately, Jersey, 2*s.*; Guernsey, 2*s.*

DAMON (Robert).—GUIDE to the GEOLOGY of WEYMOUTH and the ISLAND of PORTLAND: Containing a Map of the District, Geological Sections, Coast Views, Figures of the characteristic Fossils, and other Illustrations; with numerous Notes on the Botany and Zoology of the Coast and Neighbourhood. Fcap. 8vo, cloth, 5*s.*
   A Supplement to the above, consisting of Nine Lithographic Plates of Fossils, drawn by BONE. 2*s.* 6*d.*

DE HORSEY.—RULE OF THE ROAD AT SEA: Being PRACTICAL DIRECTIONS for complying with the BOARD of TRADE REGULATIONS for PREVENTING COLLISIONS at SEA. By CAPTAIN A. F. R. DE HORSEY, R.N., Author of 'On Manning the Navy,' 'Our Iron Navy,' &c. Fcap. 8vo, cloth, 1*s.*

DE MORGAN.—ELEMENTS of ARITHMETIC. By AUGUSTUS DE MORGAN; of Trinity College, Cambridge; Fellow of the Royal Astronomical Society, and of the Cambridge Philosophical Society; late Professor of Mathematics in University College, London. Nineteenth Thousand. Royal 12mo, cloth, 5*s.*

EAST INDIA CIVIL SERVICE EXAMINATION PAPERS, for 1867, 1866, 1865, 1864, 1860, 1859. Fcap. folio, 2s. 6d. each.

—— Further Examination Papers. 1863. Fcap. folio, 2s. 6d.

EASY LESSONS in FRENCH CONVERSATION, adapted to the topics generally interesting to Schoolboys. Demy 12mo, cloth, 1s. 6d.

EDWARDS.—STATISTICS of ALL COUNTRIES in the WORLD: Giving their Area, Form of Government, Head of State, Population, Expenditure, Debt, Paper Money, Notes in Circulation, Standing Army, Navy, Merchant Vessels, Imports, Exports, Chief Products, Money, Weights and Measures, Railways, Capitals and Chief Towns. By Dr. OTTO HÜBNER, Director of the Prussian Central Statistical Archives. The English Edition, with the sanction and co-operation of Dr. Hübner, by H. SUTHERLAND EDWARDS. One large sheet, folded, 1s.

EHRLICH.—A FRENCH METHOD, THEORETICAL and PRACTICAL; adapted to the Requirements of the University Middle-Class Examinations. By H. WM. EHRLICH, M.A., Ph.D., French Master, Royal Grammar School, Newcastle-on-Tyne. Demy 12mo, cloth, 3s. 6d.

ELLIS'S LATIN EXERCISES. Corrected by T. K. ARNOLD. 12mo, cloth, 3s. 6d.

—— KEY to the Above. 3s.

ETIENNE'S LITTLE BOY'S FIRST FRENCH BOOK: On the plan of Arnold's Henry's First Latin Book. Second Edition. Demy 12mo, cloth, 2s. 6d.

EVILL (Wm.).—A WINTER JOURNEY to ROME and BACK. With Glances at Strasburg, Milan, Florence, Naples, Pompeii, and Venice, and an Account of the Siege and Fall of Strasburg. Third Edition, with Map and Appendix. Crown 8vo, cloth, 4s. 6d.

FITCH (J. G., M.A.).—METHODS of TEACHING ARITH-METIC. A Lecture addressed to the London Association of Schoolmistresses. By J. G. FITCH, M.A., one of Her Majesty's Inspectors of Schools, and Examiner in the University of London, &c. Second Edition. Price 6d.

FITZ-GEORGE.—PLAN of the BATTLE of SEDAN, accompanied by a Short Memoir. By Captain FITZ-GEORGE, Royal Welsh Fusiliers. With Coloured Maps and Photographic Views. Demy 8vo, cloth, 12s.

FOSTER.—MANUAL of GEOGRAPHICAL PRONUNCIA-TION and ETYMOLOGY. By A. F. FOSTER, A.M., Author of 'A General Treatise on Geography,' and other Educational Works; late Editor of 'Chambers's Educational Course;' Assistant-Commissioner to the Royal Education Inquiry, &c. Seventh Edition. Fcap. 12mo, limp cloth, 2s.

This Manual furnishes Rules for the Pronunciation of the leading Languages: a Vocabulary of upwards of 10,000 Names, indicating the true Pronunciation; and an Etymological Table of Generic Terms, with their Literal Meanings, serving to explain a large number of Names.

EDWARD STANFORD, 6 & 7, CHARING CROSS, S.W.,

GILES.—The **INVASIONS** of **ENGLAND**, from the Earliest Times: A Lecture delivered before the United Service Institution, &c., &c. By Rev. Dr. GILES, C.C. Coll., Oxford. 8vo, 2s.

GILL.—**CHEMISTRY** for **SCHOOLS**: an Introduction to the Practical Study of Chemistry. By C. HAUGHTON GILL, late Assistant Examiner in Chemistry at the University of London, late Teacher of Chemistry and Experimental Physics in University College School. Second Edition, with One Hundred Illustrations. Crown 8vo, cloth, 4s. 6d.

GILL (J. W.)—**FIRST STEPS** in **ENGLISH GRAMMAR**: Compiled for the purpose of enabling Teachers to put into the hands of their Pupils a book containing only such parts as should be committed to memory. Royal 18mo, price 8d.

GODLEY.—**A SELECTION** from the **WRITINGS** and SPEECHES of JOHN ROBERT GODLEY: Collected and Edited by JAMES EDWARD FITZGERALD. Demy 8vo, half-bound, 16s.

GOOD'S (W. W.) POLITICAL, AGRICULTURAL, and **COM-**MERCIAL FALLACIES; or, the Prospects of the Nation after Twenty Years' "Free Trade." Demy 8vo, cloth, 10s. 6d.

HALL (Henry, F.R.G.S.).—**MANUAL** of **SOUTH AFRICAN** GEOGRAPHY: Forming a Companion to the Map of South Africa to 16° South Latitude. Intended for the use of the Upper Classes in Government Schools, and of Candidates for the Civil Service. Second Edition. Fcap. 8vo, cloth, 6s.

—— **SERIES** of **TECHNICAL VOCABULARIES,** in **EIGHT** LANGUAGES, comprising the leading terms in the following constructive branches:

    CIVIL AND ECCLESIASTICAL ARCHITECTURE. 2s.
    MILITARY ARCHITECTURE AND FORTIFICATION. 2s.
    CIVIL ENGINEERING AND SURVEYING. 3s.

—— (Townshend M., F.G.S.).—The **MINERALOGIST'S DIREC-**TORY; or, A GUIDE to the PRINCIPAL MINERAL LOCALITIES in the UNITED KINGDOM of GREAT BRITAIN and IRELAND. Post 8vo, cloth, 6s.

More than Seventeen Hundred Mineral Localities are noticed, and the Geological formation in which each Species occurs has been described as far as possible; whilst the various Localities are arranged Alphabetically.

HANDBOOK to **GOVERNMENT SITUATIONS**: Showing the MODE of APPOINTMENT and RATES of PAY, and containing the most RECENT REGULATIONS for OPEN COMPETITIONS for the HOME and INDIAN CIVIL SERVICES, the ENGINEERING COLLEGE, the FOREST SERVICE, and for ARMY EXAMINATIONS. With Examination Papers, and Specimens of Handwriting extracted from the Reports of the Civil Service Commissioners. Third Edition. Crown 8vo, cloth, 3s. 6d.

HULL.—COAL FIELDS of GREAT BRITAIN; their History, Structure, and Resources; with Notices of the Coal Fields of other parts of the World. By EDWARD HULL, M.A., F.R.S., Director of the Geological Survey of Ireland, Professor of Geology in the Royal College of Science, Dublin, &c. With Maps and Illustrations. Third Edition, revised and enlarged, embodying the Reports of the Royal Coal Commission. Demy 8vo, cloth. 16s.

HURLBURT.—BRITAIN and HER COLONIES. By J. B. HURLBURT, M.A., LL.D., Member of the Convocation of the University of Toronto, Canadian Commissioner and Juror at the International Exhibition, London, 1862, &c. Demy 8vo, cloth, 10s.

HUTCHINSON (T. J.).—The PARANÁ: With INCIDENTS of the PARAGUAYAN WAR, and SOUTH AMERICAN RECOLLECTIONS, from 1861 to 1868. By THOMAS J. HUTCHINSON, F.R.G.S., F.R.S.L., F.E.S., &c., H.B.M. Consul for Callao (late for Rosario); Author of 'Niger-Tshadda-Binuë Exploration;' 'Impressions of Western Africa;' 'Ten Years' Wanderings amongst the Ethiopians;' 'Buenos Ayres and Argentine Gleanings,' &c. With Map and Illustrations, including a portrait of Field-Marshal LOPEZ, the Paraguayan President. Demy 8vo, cloth, 21s.

—— **BUENOS AYRES and ARGENTINE GLEANINGS**; with Extracts from a Diary of Salado Exploration. With Maps, Illustrations, and Statistical Tables. Demy 8vo, cloth, 16s.

IRVING (C., LL.D.).—SERIES OF CATECHISMS FOR SCHOOLS. 18mo, 9d. each.
> Algebra, Part I.—Algebra, Part II.—Antiquities of Greece—Antiquities of Rome—Astronomy—Botany—British Constitution Classical Biography—Chemistry—English Grammar—French Grammar—General Geography—General Knowledge—History of England—History of France—History of Greece—History of Ireland—History of Rome—History of Scotland—Italian Grammar—Jewish Antiquities—Music—Mythology—Natural Philosophy—Practical Chemistry—Sacred History—Universal History.

JACKSON (George).—LATIN TYRO'S GUIDE; or, FIRST STEPS towards the ACQUIREMENT of LATIN. New Edition, 12mo, cloth, 1s. 6d.

—— PART II. 12mo, cloth, 1s. 6d.

JENKINSON'S PRACTICAL GUIDE to the ENGLISH LAKE DISTRICT. With Nine Maps. Contents:—Introduction—How to Spend a Flying Visit to the Lakes—a Fourteen Days' Pedestrian Tour—Charges for Conveyances, Ponies, and Guides—Heights of Mountains, Lakes, Tarns, and Passes—Local Names—Meteorology, Geology, and Botany.
> WINDERMERE, LANGDALE, GRASMERE, CONISTON, KESWICK, BUTTERMERE, WASTWATER, and ULLSWATER SECTIONS, containing full Information and Instruction respecting Walks, Drives, Boating, Ascents, Excursions, &c. Fcap. 8vo, cloth, 6s.

*** The SECTIONS relating to KESWICK and WINDERMERE (including LANGDALE) are also published separately, with Maps, price 1s. 6d. each.

EDWARD STANFORD, 6 & 7, CHARING CROSS, S.W..

JERVIS. — The **MINERAL RESOURCES** of **CENTRAL ITALY**; including Geological, Historical, and Commercial Notices of the Mines and Marble Quarries. With a Supplement, containing a Geological and Chemical Account of the whole of the Mineral Springs of Central Italy; with the best Analyses of the Waters, and Medical Notices of each Spring; compiled from the Monographs of the most esteemed writers on the subject. By W. P. JERVIS, Conservator of the Royal Italian Industrial Museum at Turin; Member of the Royal Academy of Sciences at Palermo, &c. Second Edition. Illustrated. Royal 8vo, 5s.

JEVONS (W. Stanley, M.A.). — A **SERIOUS FALL** in the VALUE of GOLD ASCERTAINED, and its Social Effects set forth. With two Diagrams. Demy 8vo, cloth, 4s.

KENNEDY. — **LA PLATA, BRAZIL,** and **PARAGUAY** DURING the WAR. By Commander A. J. KENNEDY, R.N., from Notes made while in command of H.M. Gunboat 'Spider,' during her Service on the South American Station. With Map. Post 8vo, cloth, 5s.

—— **(E. B.).** — **FOUR YEARS** in **QUEENSLAND**. With Photograph of "A Squatter's House," and a COLOURED MAP (scale, 64 miles to an inch; size, 28 inches by 18) showing all the latest Discoveries, from private and other sources, with the Agricultural Districts and Gold Fields clearly defined. Super-royal 16mo, cloth, 5s. 6d.

LANG. — **QUEENSLAND, AUSTRALIA,** the Future Cotton Field of Great Britain; with a Disquisition on the Origin, Manners, and Customs of the Aborigines. By J. D. LANG, D.D., A.M., Senior Minister of the Scots Church, Sydney, and one of the Representatives of the City of Sydney in the Parliament of New South Wales, &c. With Two Coloured Maps. Post 8vo, cloth, 12s.

LEES (Lady). — A **FEW DAYS** in **BELGIUM** and **HOLLAND**. An Idle Book for an Idle Hour. By LADY LEES, Author of 'Dried Flowers,' 'Effie's Tales,' &c. Contents:—Bruges, Ghent, Antwerp, Bruxelles, Rotterdam, the Hague, Delft, Leyden, Haarlem, Amsterdam, &c. Crown 8vo, cloth, 4s. 6d.

LEWIS. — The **ENGLISH LANGUAGE**: Its **GRAMMAR** and HISTORY; together with a TREATISE on ENGLISH COMPOSITION, and SETS of EXERCISES and EXAMINATION PAPERS for the ASSISTANCE of TEACHERS and STUDENTS. By the Rev. HENRY LEWIS, B.A., Senior Lecturer at the National Society's Training College, Battersea. Fourth Edition. Fcap. 8vo, cloth, 8s.

—— **ENGLISH GRAMMAR** for **BEGINNERS**, in a **SERIES** of EASY LESSONS. By the Rev. HENRY LEWIS, B.A., Senior Lecturer at the National Society's Training College, Battersea. Intended for the use of Junior Classes, and as an Introduction to the Author's larger English Grammar. Medium 18mo, price 2d.

LEWIS.—DIGEST OF THE ENGLISH CENSUS OF 1871, compiled from the Official Returns and Edited by JAMES LEWIS (of the Registrar-General's Department, Somerset House). Sanctioned by the Registrar-General, and dedicated by permission to the President, Vice-Presidents, and Council of the Statistical Society of London. Royal 8vo, in stiff paper covers, 4s.; or, in cloth boards, 5s.

LEY (W. Clement).—The LAWS of the WINDS PREVAILING in WESTERN EUROPE. Part I. With Synoptic Charts and Barograms; Charts of Mean Tracks of Baric Minima; of Isobarics in North Western Europe; and of the Tracks of the Great Depressions in August, 1868, and January and March, 1869. Demy 8vo, cloth, 12s.

LOBLEY (J. Logan, F.G.S.).—MOUNT VESUVIUS: A DESCRIPTIVE, HISTORICAL, and GEOLOGICAL ACCOUNT of the VOLCANO, with a NOTICE of the RECENT ERUPTION, and an Appendix, containing Letters by PLINY the Younger, a Table of Dates of Eruptions, and a List of Vesuvian Minerals. Illustrated with View, Map (printed in Colours), and Section. Demy 8vo, cloth, 5s.

LONDON and ENVIRONS.—The MULTUM in PARVO GUIDE to LONDON and its ENVIRONS, about Twenty-five Miles Round, for the Resident and the Visitor. With Cab Fares, Principal Omnibus Routes, Map of the Environs of London, &c. 18mo, cloth, 1s.

LYTTELTON'S (Lord) LECTURES on NEW ZEALAND and the CANTERBURY COLONY. 6d.

MACKIE.—GEOLOGICAL and NATURAL HISTORY REPERTORY. Volume I. An Illustrated Popular Magazine of Geology, Palæontology, Mineralogy, Zoology, and Journal of Prehistoric Archæology and Ethnology. Edited by S. J. MACKIE, F.G.S., F.S.A., F.E.S., &c. 8vo, cloth, 7s. 6d.

MANLY.—PRINCIPLES of BOOK-KEEPING by DOUBLE ENTRY, in a Series of Easy and Progressive Exercises. By HENRY MANLY, Principal Writing Master and Teacher of Book-keeping in the City of London School. Third Edition. Demy 8vo, cloth, 4s. 6d.

MARSH.—OVERLAND from SOUTHAMPTON to QUEENSLAND. By M. H. MARSH, M.A., F.R.G.S. With Three Coloured Maps. Crown 8vo, cloth, 3s. 6d.

MEMOIRS of a LIFE. Crown 8vo, cloth, 7s.

EDWARD STANFORD, 6 & 7, CHARING CROSS, S.W.,

Meteorological Office Publications.

ATLANTIC OCEAN.—A DISCUSSION of the **METEORO-**
LOGY of the PART of the ATLANTIC lying NORTH of 30° N.
for the Eleven Days ending 8th of February, 1870. By Means of
Synoptic Charts, Diagrams, and Extracts from Logs, with Remarks
and Conclusions. Published by the Authority of the METEOROLOGICAL
COMMITTEE. With Books of Charts. Royal 4to, 5s.

—— **(North).—CURRENTS and SURFACE TEMPERATURE**
of the NORTH ATLANTIC OCEAN, from the Equator to Latitude
40° N., for each Month of the Year. With a General Current Chart.
Published by the Authority of the METEOROLOGICAL COMMITTEE.
Royal 4to, 2s. 6d.

—— **METEOROLOGY of the NORTH ATLANTIC.** Report to
the COMMITTEE of the METEOROLOGICAL OFFICE, on the Meteorology of
the North Atlantic between the parallels of 40° and 50° N., as illustrated
by Eight Diagrams of Observations taken on board the Mail Steamers
running to and from America. With Remarks on the Difference in
the Winds and Weather experienced according as the ship's course is
Westerly or Easterly, and on the probable Causes of the Difference.
By Captain HENRY TOYNBEE, F.R.A.S., Marine Superintendent,
Meteorological Office. Royal 8vo, 1s.

—— **ON THE WINDS, &c., of the NORTH ATLANTIC,** along
the TRACKS of STEAMERS from the CHANNEL to NEW YORK.
Translated from No. 3 of the Mittheilungen aus der Norddeutsche See-
warte. Published by the Authority of the Meteorological Committee.
Royal 8vo, 6d.

—— **(South).—CHARTS SHOWING the SURFACE TEMPE-**
RATURE of the SOUTH ATLANTIC OCEAN in each Month of
the Year. Compiled from Board of Trade Registers, and the Charts
published by the Royal Meteorological Institute of the Netherlands.
Issued under the Authority of the COMMITTEE of the METEOROLOGICAL
OFFICE. Folio, boards, 2s. 6d.

BAROMETER MANUAL.—BOARD of TRADE. Compiled
by direction of the METEOROLOGICAL COMMITTEE. By ROBERT H.
SCOTT, M.A., F.R.S., Director of the Meteorological Office. With
Illustrative Diagrams. Royal 8vo, 1s.

CAPE HORN, &c.—CONTRIBUTIONS to our KNOWLEDGE
of the METEOROLOGY of CAPE HORN and the WEST COAST
of SOUTH AMERICA. Published by Authority of the METEORO-
LOGICAL COMMITTEE. With 12 Meteorological Charts. Royal 4to, 2s. 6d.

COAST or FISHERY BAROMETER MANUAL.—BOARD of
TRADE. Compiled under the direction of the METEOROLOGICAL
COMMITTEE. By ROBERT H. SCOTT, M.A., Director of the Meteorological
Office. 8vo, 6d.

WHOLESALE AND RETAIL BOOK AND MAP SELLER.

ISOBARIC CURVES.—On the USE of ISOBARIC CURVES, and a LINE of GREATEST BAROMETRIC CHANGE in attempting to FORETEL WINDS. Illustrated by Fourteen Diagrams of Gales in January, 1867, and August, 1868, &c. With some practical suggestions for Seamen, and a few Remarks on Buys Ballot's Law. Being a Report to the COMMITTEE of the METEOROLOGICAL OFFICE. By Captain HENRY TOYNBEE, F.R.A.S., their Marine Superintendent. Royal 8vo, 1s.

LEIPZIG CONFERENCE. — REPORT of the PROCEEDINGS of THE METEOROLOGICAL CONFERENCE at LEIPZIG, Protocols and Appendices. Published by the Authority of the Meteorological Committee. Royal 8vo, 1s.

QUARTERLY WEATHER REPORT of the METEOROLO- GICAL OFFICE, with PRESSURE and TEMPERATURE TABLES. Containing the Results of the Daily Observations made at the seven Observatories established by the Meteorological Committee at KEW, STONYHURST, FALMOUTH, ABERDEEN, GLASGOW, ARMAGH, and VALENCIA.

The Plates exhibit the continuous registration of the Observations, and are arranged to show at one view the instrumental curves at each of the stations for five days, one Plate comprising Pressure and Temperature, while another shows the Direction and Velocity of the Wind; Scales of Measurement, on both the British and French systems, being given at the sides. Published by Authority of the METEOROLOGICAL COMMITTEE. Royal 4to, price 5s. each Part.

The Parts for 1869 and 1870, also Parts I. and II., of 1871, and parts I. and II., of 1872, are now ready.

It is intended that the Journal shall appear regularly at intervals of three months.

ROUTES for STEAMERS from ADEN to the STRAITS of SUNDA AND BACK. Translated from a Paper issued by the Royal Meteorological Institute of the Netherlands. Published by the Authority of the METEOROLOGICAL COMMITTEE. Royal 8vo, 6d.

STATION INSTRUCTIONS for METEOROLOGICAL TELE- GRAPHY. 8vo, 6d.

STRONG WINDS.—An INQUIRY into the CONNECTION between STRONG WINDS and BAROMETRICAL DIFFERENCES. Being a Report presented to the COMMITTEE of the METEOROLOGICAL OFFICE. By ROBERT H. SCOTT, Director of the Office. Royal 8vo, 6d.

MEADEN. — A FIRST ALGEBRA for Use in Junior Classes. By the Rev. R. ALBAN MEADEN, M.A., late Scholar of Emmanuel College, Cambridge; Mathematical Master of the Bradford Grammar School. Fcap. 8vo, cloth, 1s. 6d.

This Work is suitable for preparing classes for the University Local Examinations, the Science Examinations, &c.

MEDHURST.—The **FOREIGNER** in **FAR CATHAY.** By W. H. MEDHURST, H.B.M. Consul, Shanghai. With Coloured Map. Crown 8vo, cloth, 6s.

CONTENTS:— Introductory — Position of Foreigners— Character and Habits of Foreign Residents — Missionaries — Consuls and Customs Authorities — Customs of the Chinese — Shop Signs — Advertising — Mandarin Yamens — Opium Smoking — Infanticide — Eating and Drinking — Social Institutions — Correspondence and the Press — Modes of Sepulture — Use of the Written Character for Decoration — Proper Names — Travelling and Porterage — Character of the Chinese — Concluding Remarks — And an Appendix, containing a Specimen of Chinese Music, with Original Words and English Literal Translation.

MILLETT (Mrs. Edward).—An **AUSTRALIAN PARSONAGE**; or, the SETTLER and the SAVAGE in WESTERN AUSTRALIA. With Frontispiece. Second Edition, Large Post 8vo, cloth, 12s.

MIMPRISS (Robt.).—**CHRIST an EXAMPLE for the YOUNG,** as EXHIBITED in the GOSPEL NARRATIVE of the FOUR EVANGELISTS. Harmonized and Chronologically Arranged, illustrated by Fifty-five Engravings, printed on different Tinted Papers to distinguish the various Periods of our Lord's Ministry, having Picture Definitions and Exercises, and a Map in Pocket. Fifth Edition. Cloth, 6s.

MINERAL STATISTICS of the **UNITED KINGDOM** of GREAT BRITAIN and IRELAND for the YEAR 1871; with an Appendix. By ROBERT HUNT, F.R.S., Keeper of the Mining Records. Published by Order of the LORDS COMMISSIONERS of HER MAJESTY'S TREASURY. Royal 8vo, 2s.

The Mineral Statistics for previous years may also be obtained.

MONGREDIEN—**ENGLAND'S FOREIGN POLICY:** An Inquiry as to whether we should continue a Policy of Intervention or adopt a Policy of Isolation. By AUGUSTUS MONGREDIEN, Esq., Author of 'Trees and Shrubs for English Plantations.' Crown 8vo, cloth, 3s. 6d.

NAUTICAL MAGAZINE. New Series. Published Monthly. 1s.

NEW ZEALAND HANDBOOK: Containing a New and Accurate Coloured Map, and giving a full description of the Provinces of Auckland, New Plymouth, Wellington, Hawkes Bay, Nelson, Marlborough, Canterbury, Otago, Southland, &c.; with Tables of Statistics, Prices, and Wages; the Land Regulations; Instructions for the Voyage, Outfit, and Arrival in the Colony; also Observations on New Zealand Pursuits and Investments. Twelfth Edition. Fcap. 8vo, 1s.

Ordnance Survey Publications, &c.

ASTRONOMICAL OBSERVATIONS made with Ramsden's Zenith Sector; together with a Catalogue of the Stars which have been observed, and the Amplitude of the Celestial Arcs, deduced from the Observations at the different Stations. 4to, sewed, 7s. 6d.

ASTRONOMICAL OBSERVATIONS made with Airey's Zenith Sector, 1842 to 1850. Completed by Captain W. YOLLAND. R.E. 20s.

DOMESDAY BOOK; or, The Great Survey of England by William the Conqueror, A.D. 1086. Facsimile of Domesday Book, reproduced by the Photozincographic Process, under the direction of Major-General Sir H. JAMES, R.E., F.R.S., by Her Majesty's Command. The following parts are already published, in imperial 4to, cloth, viz. :—

IN GREAT DOMESDAY BOOK.

			s.	d.					s.	d.
Bedfordshire	.. ...	price	8	0	Leicestershire and Rutland					
Berkshire ..	.. ..	„	8	0			price	8	0
Buckingham	.. ..	„	8	0	Lincolnshire	.. ..	„	21	0
Cambridge	.. ..	„	10	0	Middlesex..	.. ..	„	8	0
Cheshire and Lancashire	„		8	0	Nottinghamshire	.. ..	„	10	0
Cornwall ..	.. ..	„	8	0	Northamptonshire	..	„	8	0
Derbyshire	.. ..	„	8	0	Oxfordshire	.. ..	„	8	0
Devonshire	.. ..	„	10	0	Rutlandshire (bound with				
Dorsetshire	.. ..	„	8	0	Leicestershire)	..	„	8	0
Gloucestershire	..	„	8	0	Shropshire	.. ..	„	8	0
Hampshire	.. ..	„	10	0	Somersetshire	.. ..	„	10	0
Herefordshire ..	..	„	8	0	Staffordshire	.. ..	„	8	0
Hertfordshire ..	..	„	10	0	Surrey	.. .. ..	„	8	0
Huntingdon	.. ..	„	8	0	Sussex	.. .. ..	„	10	0
Kent	..	„	8	0	Warwickshire	.. ..	„	8	0
Lancashire (see Cheshire					Wiltshire ..	.. ..	„	10	0
and Lancashire) ..	„	8	0	Worcestershire..	..	„	8	0
					Yorkshire..	.. ..	„	21	0

IN LITTLE DOMESDAY BOOK.

Essex, price 16s.—Norfolk, 23s.—Suffolk, 22s.

Price of an entire Set (as above), 17l. 3s.

Domesday Book complete, bound in 2 volumes, price 20l.

EDWARD STANFORD, 6 & 7, CHARING CROSS, S.W.,

GEODETICAL TABLES. 1 vol., thin 4to, price 2s.

JERUSALEM.—ORDNANCE SURVEY of JERUSALEM,
With Notes by Captain WILSON, R.E. Produced at the Ordnance Survey Office, Southampton, under the superintendence of Major-General Sir HENRY JAMES, R.E., F.R.S., Director.

The Survey is sold complete for Twelve Guineas, or in Divisions, as follows:—

	£	s.	d.
The Plans Mounted, and in a Portfolio	2	18	0
Vol. I. Containing Captain Wilson's Notes on Jerusalem, and Illustrative Diagrams	2	0	0
Vol. II. Containing the Photographs taken in and about the City	7	14	0
Total	£12	12	0

The Plans, Diagrams, and Photographs are sold separately. Detailed List, with Prices, post free for two Penny Stamps.

LENGTH.—COMPARISONS of the STANDARDS of LENGTH
of England, France, Belgium, Prussia, Russia, India, Australia, made at the Ordnance Survey Office, Southampton, by Captain A. R. CLARKE, R.E., F.R.S., under the direction of Major-General Sir HENRY JAMES, R.E., F.R.S., &c., Cor. Mem. of the Royal Geographical Society of Berlin, Director of the Ordnance Survey. Published by Order of the Secretary of State for War. 1 vol. 4to, 287 pp. and plates. Price 15s.

LOUGH FOYLE BASE.—An ACCOUNT of the MEASURE-
MENTS of the LOUGH FOYLE BASE. By Captain W. YOLLAND, R.E. 4to, cloth, 20s.

MAGNA CARTA.—KING JOHN, A.D. 1215. Facsimile of Magna Carta; Photozincographed at the Ordnance Survey Office, Southampton, under the superintendence of Captain PARSONS, R.E., F.R.A.S. Price 1s. 6d., with the Translation.

MARGINAL LINES.—On the CONSTRUCTION and USE of
the SIX SHEETS of MARGINAL LINES for MAPS of any part of the WORLD. Price 1s.

⁎ The Six Sheets of Marginal Lines are published, price 6s.

METEOROLOGICAL OBSERVATIONS, TABLES for. Published separately, in 1 vol. royal 8vo, price 2s. 6d.

DITTO taken at the Stations of the Royal Engineers in the Years 1853 to 1859. 1 vol. 4to, price 10s. 6d.

METEROLOGICAL OBSERVATIONS, taken at the Stations of the Royal Engineers, 1853–4. 1 vol. 4to, price 2s. 6d.

DITTO taken at Dublin. 1 vol. 4to, price 5s.

DITTO taken at the Royal Engineer's Office, New Westminster, British Columbia, in 1860–1. Price 1s.

NATIONAL MANUSCRIPTS of ENGLAND. A Series of PHOTOZINCOGRAPHIC FACSIMILES of some of the most interesting of our National MSS., copied by order of Her Majesty's Government, by Major-General Sir HENRY JAMES, R.E., F.R.S., Director of the Ordnance Survey; with Translations and Introductory Notes by W. BASEVI SANDERS, Esq., Assistant Keeper of Her Majesty's Records. This series, consisting of Royal Charters and Grants, and the Letters of Royal and Eminent or Remarkable Persons, has been selected under the direction of the Right Hon. Sir JOHN ROMILLY, Master of the Rolls; by THOMAS DUFFUS HARDY, Esq., Deputy Keeper of Her Majesty's Records; and includes some of the most remarkable Original Documents deposited in Her Majesty's Record Office, together with a few from other repositories, including the most perfect Original Copy of Magna Carta now extant. They are not only of the highest historical interest, but at the same time illustrate the changes which have successively occurred in our language and handwriting from the reign of William the Conqueror to the reign of Queen Anne. The Facsimiles are arranged chronologically, and the Translations are interleaved so as to appear opposite to each page of the Facsimile of the Original Manuscripts. The series is published in Four Parts, price 16s. each.

—— **SCOTLAND.**—Photozincographic Facsimiles of National Manuscripts of Scotland. Part II. Price 21s. Part I. out of print.

NETLEY ABBEY—PHOTOZINCOGRAPHED VIEWS OF. Sixteen Photographic Views, &c., of Netley Abbey, including illustrated Title Page and Plan of the Abbey. Photozincographed at the Ordnance Survey Office, Southampton. Major-General Sir HENRY JAMES, R.E., F.R.S. (Director). Price complete, in a neat portfolio, 25s.

These Views have been selected expressly for the purpose of showing the applicability of the Art of Photozincography or Photolithography to the production of illustrations of historical or descriptive works of any kind. The negatives, the silver prints, and the photozincographs are absolutely untouched. The title page, the plan, and the note have also been printed by photozincography.

EDWARD STANFORD, 6 & 7, CHARING CROSS, S.W.,
16.

ORDNANCE TRIGONOMETRICAL SURVEY of the UNITED

KINGDOM. In Four Volumes, royal 4to, illustrated with numerous Plates, bound in cloth, 3l. 5s. The Account of this Survey is now complete, and may be had as above, or in separate volumes as under :—

I. THE PRINCIPAL TRIANGULATION of the UNITED KINGDOM, with the Figure, Dimensions, and Mean Specific Gravity of the Earth as derived therefrom. With Plates, 1l. 15s.

APPENDIX TO DITTO.—Determination of the Positions of Feaghmain and Haverfordwest, Longitude Stations on the great European Arc of Parallel. 4to, price 4s. 6d.

II. THE LEVELLING TAKEN IN ENGLAND AND WALES. With Plates, 15s.

III. THE LEVELLING TAKEN IN SCOTLAND. With Plates, 10s.

IV. THE LEVELLING TAKEN IN IRELAND. Price 5s.

*** The Volumes of Levelling will be found of great value to all Engineers, Geologists, and Scientific Persons, as they contain the Lines of Levels taken throughout the Kingdom, and give the exact height of every Bench Mark or Bolt, or other object observed above the mean level of the sea.

SINAI.—ORDNANCE SURVEY of SINAI. This Survey is

published in Three Parts, and sold complete for 22l.

The Parts can also be had separately as follows :—

Part I. DESCRIPTIVE ACCOUNT AND ILLUSTRATIONS. —The Origin, Progress, and Results of the Survey, with twenty pages of Illustrations. In 1 Volume, imperial folio, half-bound, price 4l.

Part II. MAPS.—This Part consists of Ten Maps and Sections of the Peninsula of Sinai, Mount Sinai, and Mount Serbál, mounted on cloth to fold. With portfolio, price 5l. Single Maps can be had if required.

Part III. PHOTOGRAPHS.—The Photographs taken to illustrate the Ordnance Survey of Sinai are published in 3 Vols., half-bound in morocco, price 13l.; or separately, price, Vol. I., 5l. 5s.; Vol. II., 5l. 5s.; Vol. III., 2l. 10s. Any of the Photographs (numbering 153) may be purchased separately at the following prices, viz. those in Vols. I. and II., unmounted, 1s., mounted, 1s. 6d. each; those in Vol. III., unmounted, 9d., mounted, 1s. each.

— ONE HUNDRED and ELEVEN ADDITIONAL PHO-
TOGRAPHS are also published, and may be purchased separately; price 1s. each unmounted; or 1s. 6d. mounted.

— STEREOSCOPIC VIEWS, Thirty-six in number, in a Box-Stereoscope. Price Two Guineas.

A Detailed List of the Photographs and List of Maps sent by post for Two Penny Stamps.

SPHERE and SPHEROID.—On the Rectangular Tangential Projection of the Sphere and Spheroid, with Tables of the quantities requisite for the construction of Maps on that Projection ; and also for a Map of the World on the scale of ten miles to an inch, with Diagrams and Outline Map. By Major-General Sir HENRY JAMES, R.E., F.R.S., &c. Price 8s. 6d.

STONEHENGE, TURUSACHAN, CROMLECHS, and SCULP-TURED STONES. Plans and Photographs; with Descriptions and Notes relating to the Druids. Also an Appendix on some Sculptured Stones recently found in Ireland; accompanied by Plates. By Major-General Sir HENRY JAMES, R.E., F.R.S. 1 vol. 4to, cloth, price 14s. 6d.

Photograph of Stonehenge Restored, showing Druidical Sacrifice by Night. Price 1s. 3d. unmounted; 1s. 9d. mounted.

PALESTINE EXPLORATION FUND PHOTOGRAPHS. PHOTOGRAPHIC VIEWS of PALESTINE, taken expressly for the Palestine Exploration Fund in 1865, 1866, 1867. By Sergeant H. PHILLIPS, R.E., under the orders of Captain WILSON, R.E., and Lieutenant WARREN, R.E.

This beautiful series of Original Photographs now comprises 356 most interesting Views of the Cities, Villages, Temples, Synagogues, Churches, Ruins, Tombs, Seas, Lakes, Priests, Pilgrims, Inhabitants, &c., of the Holy Land and Jerusalem. Any Photograph may be had separately. Mounted on a white board, size 13 inches by 11, price 1s. 6d. each; or, a Selection of 14 Photographs, in cloth portfolio, lettered, 21s. A List of the Views gratis on application, or per post for penny stamp. Descriptive Catalogue, 6d.

PARTRIDGE.—The **MAKING of the AMERICAN NATION**; or, The Rise and Decline of Oligarchy in the West. By J. ARTHUR PARTRIDGE, Author of 'Coalitions and Frontiers in 1860-1;' 'The False Nation and its Basis;' 'Democracy,' &c. Demy 8vo, cloth, 16s.

PAUL (Archdeacon).—**NEW ZEALAND AS IT WAS and AS IT IS.** With Map. Fcap. 8vo, 6d.

PERIGAL (F.).—The **YEAR 1800**; or, The Sayings and Doings of our Fathers and Mothers 70 Years ago, as recorded in the Newspapers and other Periodicals. Third Edition. Super-royal 8vo, 1s. 6d.

PHILPOT.—**GUIDE BOOK to the CANADIAN DOMINION**: Containing full information for the Emigrant, the Tourist, the Sportsman, and the small Capitalist. Dedicated, by permission, to His Royal Highness Prince Arthur. By HARVEY J. PHILPOT, M.D. (Canada), M.R.C.S.L., &c., late Assistant-Surgeon to Her Majesty's Forces in Turkey and the Crimea. With a Preface by THOMAS HUGHES, Esq., M.P., and a COLOURED MAP. Super-royal 16mo, cloth, 4s.

PLATTS' (Rev. J.) DICTIONARY of ENGLISH SYNO-NYMES: Comprehending the Derivations and Meanings of the Words, and the Distinctions between the Synonymes; with Examples. New Edition. Demy 12mo, 3s. 6d.

PLŒTZ.—MANUEL DE LA LITTÉRATURE FRANÇAISE des XVIIE, XVIIIE, et XIXE Siècles. Par O. PLŒTZ, Docteur en Philosophie, ancient Premier Professeur au Collége Français de Berlin. Seconde Edition, Revue et Augmentée. Demy 8vo, cloth, 6s. 6d.

POOR RELIEF IN DIFFERENT PARTS OF EUROPE: being a Selection of Essays, translated from the German Work, 'Das Armenwesen und die Armengesetzgebung in Europäischen Staaten herausgegeben,' Von A. Emminghaus. Revised by E. B. EASTWICK, C.B., M.P. Crown 8vo, cloth, 7s.

POPE.—A CLASS BOOK of RUDIMENTARY CHEMISTRY. By the Rev. GEO. POPE, M.A., Fellow of Sidney Sussex College, Cambridge, and one of the Masters of the College, Hurstpierpoint. 18mo, stiff cover, 9d.

RAMSAY.—PHYSICAL GEOLOGY and GEOGRAPHY of GREAT BRITAIN. By A. C. RAMSAY, LL.D., F.R.S., &c., Director-General of the Geological Surveys of the United Kingdom. Third Edition, considerably enlarged, and illustrated with NUMEROUS SECTIONS and a GEOLOGICAL MAP of GREAT BRITAIN, printed in Colours. Post 8vo, cloth, 7s. 6d.

"This, the third edition, has been partly rewritten, and contains much new matter. . . . . The preliminary sketch of the different formations, and of the phenomena connected with the metamorphism of rocks, has been much enlarged; and many long and important paragraphs have been added in the chapters on the physical structure of England and Scotland—partly on subjects connected with the coal question, partly on the glacial epoch, partly on the union of Britain with the Continent at various epochs, and the migrations of animals hither; and on many other subjects. An entire new chapter has been added on the origin of the river courses of Britain; and large additions have been made to the earlier brief account of soils, and the economic products of the various geological formations. There are also many new illustrative sections."—*Extract from Preface.*

—— **GEOLOGY of NORTH WALES.** By A. C. RAMSAY, LL.D., F.R.S., Director-General of the Geological Surveys of the United Kingdom. With Map and Sections; and an Appendix on the Fossils, with Plates, by J. W. SALTER, A.L.S., F.G.S., late Palæontologist to the Survey. Royal 8vo, cloth, 13s.

*** This work is published by Order of the Lords Commissioners of Her Majesty's Treasury, and forms Volume III. of the 'Memoirs of the Geological Survey of Great Britain.'

RAVENSTEIN. — **DENOMINATIONAL STATISTICS OF ENGLAND AND WALES.** By E. G. RAVENSTEIN, F.R.G.S., &c. Topographical and Statistical Department, War Office. Crown 8vo, cloth, 1s. 6d.

READING DISENTANGLED; or, Classified Lessons in Spelling and Reading. By the Author of 'Peep of Day,' &c. With Frontispiece and Upwards of One Hundred and Fifty Illustrations. New Edition. Cloth, lettered, 2s. 6d.

REYNOLDS (Geo.).—EXERCISES in ARITHMETIC; with a copious variety of Bills of Parcels. Intended as an Auxiliary Companion to every Treatise on Practical and Commercial Arithmetic. 12mo, cloth, 2s. 6d.

—— **KEY to Ditto.** 12mo, 2s.

ROBSON (J., B.A.).—CONSTRUCTIVE LATIN EXERCISES, for Teaching the Elements of the Language on a System of Analysis and Synthesis, with Latin Reading Lessons and copious Vocabularies. By JOHN ROBSON, B.A., Lond., Secretary of University College, London, formerly Classical Master in University College School. Eighth Edition. 12mo, cloth, 4s. 6d.

—— **CONSTRUCTIVE GREEK EXERCISES,** for Teaching the Elements of the Language on a System of Analysis and Synthesis, with Greek Reading Lessons and copious Vocabularies. By JOHN ROBSON, B.A., Lond., Secretary of University College, London, formerly Classical Master in University College School. 12mo, cloth, 7s. 6d.

The plan of this Book is as nearly as possible the same as that of the Author's 'Latin Exercises.'

—— **FIRST GREEK BOOK.** Containing Exercises and Reading Lessons on the Inflexions of Substantives and Adjectives, and of the Active Verb in the Indicative Mood. With copious Vocabularies. Being the First Part of the Constructive Greek Exercises. Second Edition. 12mo, cloth, 3s. 6d.

SCHOOL-BOYS' LETTERS for COPYING and DICTATION: being a Series of Lithographed Letters on Subjects interesting to School-Boys, with Remarks on the Essentials of Good Writing, &c. Second Edition. Large post 8vo, cloth, 2s. 6d.

SCHOOL REGISTERS.—HALBRAKE REGISTER of AT-TENDANCE and STUDIES. Designed for Private and Middle Class Schools. Demy 8vo, coloured wrapper, 8d.

SCHOOL REGISTERS.—LONDON CLASS-REGISTER and SUMMARY OF ATTENDANCE and PAYMENTS. A New and Improved Edition. Adapted to the requirements of the "New Code." By WILLIAM RICE, F.R.G.S., Author of the 'Class and Home Lesson Book of English History.' Fcap. folio, 1s.

SCHOOL PUNISHMENT REGISTER. — The **LONDON** SCHOOL REGISTER of PUNISHMENTS. Designed to meet the Requirements of School Boards, &c. Fcap. folio, stiff boards, cloth back, 2s. 6d.

SCOTT (J. R.). — The **FAMILY GUIDE to BRUSSELS**: Comprising Hints upon Hiring Houses, Furniture, Servants, Cost of Living, Education, and the General Information necessary for a Family purposing to reside in that city. By J. R. SCOTT, of Brussels. Crown 8vo, cloth, gilt, 4s.

SIMMS. — The **FIRST SIX BOOKS of the ILIAD of HOMER,** Translated into Fourteen Syllable Verse, with Preface and Notes, and a Map of Greece in the Homeric Age. Designed as a Reading Book for Colleges and Schools. By the Rev. EDWARD SIMMS, M.A., Oxon., Vicar of Escot, Devon. Demy 8vo, cloth, 7s. 6d.

SKEEN. — **ADAM'S PEAK**: LEGENDARY, TRADITIONAL, and HISTORIC NOTICES of the SAMANALA and SRÍ-PÁDA; with a Descriptive Account of the PILGRIMS' ROUTE FROM COLOMBO TO THE SACRED FOOT-PRINT. By WILLIAM SKEEN, Member of the Ceylon Branch of the Royal Asiatic Society. With Map. Fcap. 4to, cloth, 10s. 6d.

—— **MOUNTAIN LIFE and COFFEE CULTIVATION in** CEYLON; a Poem on the KNUCKLES RANGE, with other Poems. By WILLIAM SKEEN, Member of the Ceylon Branch of the Royal Asiatic Society. Fcap. 4to, cloth, 7s.

STATISTICAL SOCIETY. — **JOURNAL of the STATISTICAL** SOCIETY of LONDON. Published Quarterly, price 5s. Complete Sets, from the Year 1838 to December, 1872, can be had, with General Index up to 1862, price 22l. 12s.

STOCQUELER. — **A FAMILIAR HISTORY of the BRITISH** ARMY, from the Restoration in 1660 to the Present Time, including a Description of the Volunteer Movement, and the Progress of the Volunteer Organization. By J. H. STOCQUELER, Author of an 'Illustrated Life of the Duke of Wellington,' 'The Military Encyclopædia,' 'The Old Field Officer,' 'The British Soldier,' 'The Volunteers' Handbook,' &c. Crown 4to, cloth, 21s.

SULLIVAN (Sir Edward, Bart.). — **TEN CHAPTERS on** SOCIAL REFORM. Demy 8vo, cloth, price 5s.

CONTENTS.

Reform. — The Working Classes. — The Church. — The Residuum. — Pauperism, &c. — Drunkenness, &c. — Crime, &c. — Education. — Demagogues. — Objects of Radical Politicians, &c.

SULLIVAN (Sir Edward, Bart.).—PROTECTION to NATIVE
INDUSTRY. By Sir EDWARD SULLIVAN, Bart., Author of 'Ten Chapters on Social Reform.' Demy 8vo, cloth, 5s.

CONTENTS.

Growth of Trade. — Free Trade and Free Ports. — Corn. — Special Interests. — Producer and Consumer. — Unfair Competition. — Labour. — Cotton. — French Treaty. — Board of Trade Statistics. — Reciprocity. — Causes and Remedies.

Appendix.—The Worsted Trade and the French Treaty—Intoxicating Liquor the National Curse.

SYMONS.—BRITISH RAINFALL, 1872. The DISTRIBU-TION of RAIN over the BRITISH ISLES during the YEAR 1872, as observed at about 1700 Stations in Great Britain and Ireland. With REMARKS on VARIOUS EXPERIMENTS, MAPS, and ILLUSTRATIONS. Compiled by G. J. SYMONS, F.M.S., F.R.B.S., Member of the Scottish Meteorological Society, &c. Demy 8vo, cloth, 5s. [*Published Annually.*

—— **RAIN: HOW, WHEN, WHERE, and WHY** it is MEASURED; being a Popular Account of Rainfall Investigations. With Illustrations. By G. J. SYMONS, F.M.S., Editor of 'British Rainfall,' &c. This work is intended to serve a double purpose—to be a manual for the use of observers, and to provide the public at large with an epitome of the results hitherto obtained, and their application to the wants of civilized life. It also contains interesting particulars of the Rainfall in all parts of the world. Post 8vo, cloth, 2s.

—— The **MONTHLY METEOROLOGICAL MAGAZINE.** Vol. I. to VI. Demy 8vo, cloth, price 5s. each. Published in Monthly Parts, 4d. each.

—— **REGISTRATION FORMS.**—Forms for One Year, with Instructions, in stiff cover, 2s.
Forms for Five Years, with Instructions, half-bound, 7s. 6d.

—— **BAROMETER DIAGRAMS.**—Set of 12 for One Year. 1s.

TOOGOOD (Mrs.).—SIMPLE SKETCHES from CHURCH HISTORY, for YOUNG PERSONS. New Edition. 18mo, cloth, 1s. 6d.

VICTORIA, The BRITISH "EL DORADO." Showing the advantages of that Colony as a field for Emigration. By a COLONIST of Twenty Years' Standing, and late Member of a Colonial Legislature. With Two Coloured Views and a Map. Super-royal 16mo, cloth, 5s. 6d.

WALLACE'S (W.) MINERAL DEPOSITS.—The Laws which Regulate the Deposition of Lead Ore in Mineral Lodes. Illustrated by an Examination of the Geological Structure of the Mining Districts of Alston Moor. With Map and numerous Coloured Plates. Large demy 8vo, cloth, 25s.

EDWARD STANFORD, 6 & 7, CHARING CROSS, S.W.,

WEBBER.—THE KAIETEUR FALLS, BRITISH GUIANA.
THE ESSEQUIBO and POTARO RIVERS. With an Account of a Visit to the recently discovered Kaieteur Falls. By LIEUT.-COLONEL WEBBER, 2nd West India Regiment. With Map and Frontispiece, and Descriptive Notes on the Geology of Guiana. Crown 8vo, cloth, 4s. 6d.

WELD.—HINTS to INTENDING SHEEP FARMERS in
NEW ZEALAND. By FREDERICK A. WELD, New Zealand, Member of the House of Representatives, &c. With an Appendix on the Land Regulations. Fcap. 8vo, 8d.

WHITAKER.—The GEOLOGY of the LONDON BASIN.
Part I. The Chalk and the Eocene Beds of the Southern and Western Tracts. By W. WHITAKER, B.A. Parts by H. W. BRISTOW, F.R.S., and T. McK. HUGHES, M.A. Royal 8vo, cloth, 13s.

₊ This work is published by Order of the Lords Commissioners of Her Majesty's Treasury, and forms Volume IV. of the 'Memoirs of the Geological Survey of Great Britain.'

WILKINS.—The GEOLOGY and ANTIQUITIES of the ISLE
of WIGHT. By Dr. E. P. WILKINS, F.G.S., &c. To which is added the Topography of the Island—so condensed as to give all that is useful to the Tourist — by JOHN BRION. It is illustrated by an elaborately-executed Relievo Map of the Island, coloured geologically; by numerous finely-engraved geological sections; and by a fine lithograph in colours of the tessalated pavements of the Roman Villa lately discovered at Carisbrooke. Super-royal 8vo, cloth, 7s. 6d.

WYATT.—REFLECTIONS on the FORMATION of ARMIES,
with a VIEW to the RE-ORGANIZATION of the ENGLISH ARMY. Together with a TRANSLATION of the ARCHDUKE ALBRECHT'S celebrated Pamphlet on the 'RESPONSIBILITY in TIMES of WAR.' By Captain W. J. WYATT (Unattached), formerly of the Radetzky Hussars, Author of 'A Political and Military Review of the Austro-Italian War, 1866,' &c. Royal 8vo, stitched, 3s.

WYATT.—A POLITICAL and MILITARY HISTORY of the
HANOVERIAN and ITALIAN WAR. With Maps and Plans. Royal 8vo, 10s. 6d.

—— A POLITICAL and MILITARY REVIEW of the
AUSTRO-ITALIAN WAR of 1866, with an Account of the Garibaldian Expedition to the Tyrol: a Review of the Future Policy of Italy, and her Present Financial Difficulties. With Photographic Portrait of the Archduke Albrecht. Demy 8vo, cloth, 6s.

YOUNG.—READABLE SHORT-HAND—SELF-TAUGHT:
Being a System by which people can teach themselves, write the longest word without lifting the pen, read what they write, and correspond with friends at home or abroad on pleasure or business. It embraces a double set of vowels, with Liquid Consonants grafted on the other letters; together with a DIAGRAM of DOTS, and a Combination of Words in most familiar use into ready sentences. The whole forming a SYSTEM of READABLE SHORT-HAND, SHORTENED. By MURDO YOUNG. Demy 12mo, boards, 2s. 6d.

CATALOGUES

ISSUED BY

EDWARD STANFORD,

6 and 7, CHARING CROSS, LONDON, S.W.

1. **GENERAL CATALOGUE of ATLASES, MAPS, GLOBES,** &c., published or sold by EDWARD STANFORD. New Edition.

1.* **BOOKS.**—Selected List of Books published by EDWARD STANFORD.

3. **ORDNANCE MAPS.**—Catalogue of the Ordnance Maps, published under the superintendence of Major-General Sir HENRY JAMES, R.E., F.R.S., Superintendent of the Ordnance Surveys. Price 6d.; per post, 7d.

4. **GEOLOGICAL SURVEY of GREAT BRITAIN and IRE-**LAND.—Catalogue of the Geological Maps, Sections, and Memoirs of the Geological Survey of Great Britain and Ireland, under the superintendence of Professor RAMSAY, LL.D., F.R.S., Director-General of the Geological Surveys of the United Kingdom.

5. **GEOLOGICAL MAPS in general.**—Catalogue of the best Geological Maps of various parts of the World.

6. **MAPS of LONDON and its ENVIRONS.**

7. **USEFUL KNOWLEDGE MAPS.**—Catalogue of Atlases, Maps, and Plans, engraved under the superintendence of THE SOCIETY FOR THE DIFFUSION OF USEFUL KNOWLEDGE.

8. **ADMIRALTY CHARTS.**—Catalogue of Charts, Plans, Views, and Sailing Directions, &c., published by order of the Lords Commissioners of THE ADMIRALTY. 200 pages, royal 8vo. Price 3s.; per post, 3s. 3d.

10. **SCHOOL STATIONERY.**—STANFORD's Catalogue and Specimens of School Stationery, with Lists of Educational Books, Atlases, Maps, and Globes.

10.* **SPECIAL LIST of EDUCATIONAL WORKS,** selected from the Publications of Edward Stanford, including those formerly published by Varty and Cox.

11. **SCHOOL PRIZE BOOKS.**—List of Works specially adapted for Schools, Prizes, Awards, and Presentations.

13. **BOOKS and MAPS for TOURISTS.**—STANFORD's Tourist's Catalogue, containing a list, irrespective of publisher, of all the best Books and Maps suitable for the British and Continental Traveller.

15. **MILITARY, NAVAL, and OFFICIAL BOOKS for the** Army and Navy.

16. **SAMPLES of GENERAL STATIONERY, with Prices** attached.

19. **CLEARANCE CATALOGUE.**—Stanford's Clearance Catalogue of Standard and Popular Works, Atlases, &c., offered at a considerable reduction from the published prices.

₊ With the exception of Nos. 3 and 8, any of the above can be had gratis on application, or per post for one penny stamp.

EDWARD STANFORD, 6 & 7, CHARING CROSS, S.W.